The big book
of
team coaching games

The big book

of

team coaching games

Quick, Effective Activities to Energize, Motivate, and
Guide Your Team to Success

Mary Scannell
Mike Mulvihill
Joanne Schlosser

New York   Chicago   San Francisco   Lisbon   London   Madrid   Mexico City
Milan   New Delhi   San Juan   Seoul   Singapore   Sydney   Toronto

1   2   3   4   5   6   7   8   9   0   QFR/QFR   1   9   8   7   6   5   4   3

ISBN   978-0-07-181300-6
MHID   0-07-181300-4

e-ISBN   978-0-07-181301-3
e-MHID   0-07-181301-2

McGraw-Hill Education books are available at special quantity discounts to use as premiums and sales promotions or for use in corporate training programs. To contact a representative, please visit the Contact Us pages at www.mhprofessional.com.

This book is printed on acid-free paper.

Contents

Acknowledgments

Thank you to all the teams we have had the pleasure of working with over the years, and to all the leaders, coaches, and mentors who carry on the good work of helping individuals and teams become the best they can be. This book is dedicated to you.

We would like to thank Casie Vogel and Donya Dickerson, our editors at McGraw-Hill, for inviting us once again to contribute to the Big Book series. We are grateful for your support and confidence in us. Thanks also to Moe Dennehy at McGraw-Hill for her dedication to the Big Book series. To Laura Yieh, our marketing wizard at McGraw-Hill, thank you for your work in promoting the book.

A special thanks to everyone involved in the production of this book, including Maureen Harper at McGraw-Hill and the incomparable Rena Copperman and her team. Rena, it has been a joy working with you and copy editor extraordinaire Carolyn Wendt once again. We are grateful to you for your hard work, expertise, and friendship.

It's been a pleasure working with all of you!

On a personal note, thank you to Mike and Joanne—two gifted coaches I am lucky to call friends. I would like to thank my dad, Ed, for showing me what it truly looks like to pay it forward, and my mom, Alice, for showing me how to approach any job with energy and enthusiasm. Thank you to Cathie, for teaching me to live courageously. And to Karen, thank you for sharing your beautiful spirit. A special thanks to Coach "Iron Mike" Scannell, who is one of the greatest coaches I know. You exemplify what it means to be a coach in your attitude and your actions and you make a difference every day to so many of us.

—Mary Scannell

A big "Huzzah!" to my coauthors Mary Scannell and Joanne Schlosser for the hard work, expertise, and spirit of fun they brought to the making of this book. It has been a wonderful privilege working with you both.

I would like to thank my family for their love and encouragement, not only during the writing of this book, but throughout my life. I would also like to offer a special thanks to my wife, Chrissy, for her love and support, and for the many ways she inspires me and so many others as a coach, friend, and teacher.

—Mike Mulvihill

Thank you to my family and especially to Rick for his love and support. Thank you to Mary and Mike for inviting me to collaborate. Thank you to all the great coaches and yoga teachers who've educated and encouraged me to be my best self and to help others reach their full potential. Thank you to my wonderful clients who teach and stretch me as we work together to achieve amazing outcomes.

—Joanne Schlosser

1

What Is Team Coaching?

Coaching works, and because it works we will continue to see it grow and evolve for many years to come.

—Rich Fettke

Team Coaching Games

This book is meant to be a resource for a coach or facilitator. These team coaching games can be played to help build team cohesiveness, break the ice, and prepare the team to move forward together. The team coaching games in this book provide ideas and activities you can incorporate into your team coaching efforts. They range from verbal activities to physical activities and can take anywhere from a few minutes to an hour or longer. Each game comes with complete instructions including how many people can participate and any supplies you will need or advance preparations you will want to make. As the coach, please review the Objectives and Setting the Context sections of each game to determine which games will best serve the specific objective you wish to accomplish.

Teams that have fun together are better able to retain the learning, break down barriers, and build stronger relationships. The discussion questions are useful in guiding the conversation to debrief the activity, to verbalize the lessons learned, and, where appropriate, to discuss how to take the learning back to work to help the team move forward.

Who Is This Book For?

This is not a how-to manual for becoming a coach. This book is designed for people who are already experienced coaches, who have some experience in team coaching or are team or group facilitators, and who are comfortable in the role.

The coach can be an internal resource for the organization or an external resource. There are many organizations worldwide that certify coaches. The International Coach Federation (www.coachfederation.org) is the best known with over 21,000 members in 110 countries worldwide. A certified coach has training in basic coaching skills and has met some specific criteria to serve as a coach.

The three levels of certification recognized by the International Coach Federation are:

- Associate Certified Coach (ACC), which requires a minimum of 60 hours of coaching education and a minimum of 100 hours of coaching experience.
- Professional Certified Coach (PCC), which requires a minimum of 125 hours of coaching education and a minimum of 750 hours of coaching experience.
- Master Certified Coach (MCC), which requires a minimum of 200 hours of coaching education and a minimum of 2,500 hours of coaching experience.

Each of the above credentials has additional requirements.

Not all coaches have facilitation skills training or work with teams. Not all facilitators are trained coaches. Ideally, the person leading these team coaching games is a coach who is skilled at coaching and facilitating teams.

Our Definition of Team Coaching

Team coaching is a means to accelerate the team development process. Team coaching means working with an intact team to develop and/or accelerate the ability of the team to work together to achieve results. The coach also usually provides one-on-one coaching to the team leader to help the leader achieve the desired results in the most effective way. The goal is to improve the quality of communication and relationships while creating a clear vision of the future so the team can move together in the desired direction to accomplish their task(s).

Using a formal process for team coaching accelerates the results a team might achieve and works to hold the team members accountable for their results and their commitments to one another. Team coaching enables ideas and improvements toward team goals to be worked on and shared in real time, because learning, action, and cooperation are integrated into the team journey and outcomes.

Our Definition of Team Building

Team building refers to the various activities undertaken to build rapport among the team members and increase the overall performance of the team. You can't expect that team members will perform on their own; they need communication, trust, and a vision of where they are going. Team-building activities consist of various tasks and games that will work to strengthen the bond among the team members toward one another and toward the achievement of their objective.

Team building is an element of team coaching. Team coaching provides more of a big picture approach and incorporates elements of team building, coaching, and facilitation to ensure the team reaches its goals. Figure 1 shows how the components intersect and interrelate. For more information on the stages of team and group development, look at Chapter 3. Understanding these will enable team members to recognize their current stage and help them progress to the next stage more readily.

Our Definition of Coaching

Coaching is a focused, transformational process that supports self-discovery, change, and action. It is an empowering way of relating to others that allows them to find the answers for themselves. Coaching can be provided to an individual, team, or group.

Our Definition of Facilitation

Facilitation is provided by one or more individuals who can remain neutral while working to keep an agenda on track in order to ensure that all voices at a meeting are heard, to bring forth new ideas, and/or to move actions forward. Teams often benefit from the skills of a formally trained facilitator for this reason. Alternatively, different team members may take turns facilitating to ensure that everyone has a chance to participate fully, when not serving as facilitator. Facilitation may be a onetime event but is most effective over a period of time. The same facilitator, from within or outside the organization, may work with a team or group over time to focus the group on identifying and achieving results. Facilitators are often used for important business meetings, strategic planning sessions, and retreats.

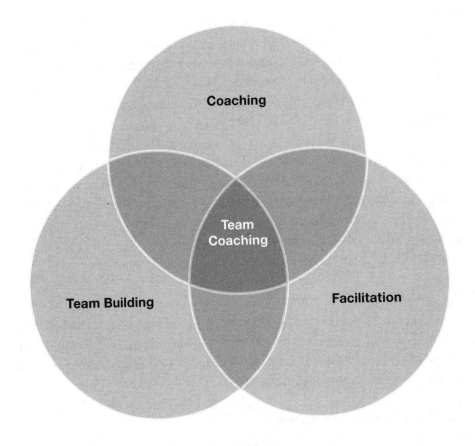

Figure 1 Team Coaching Model
© 2013 Schlosser, Scannell, Mulvihill

Skills for Effective Coaching

The International Coach Federation (ICF) has a terrific list of the eleven coaching competencies they believe every coach should possess. Here, we are choosing to highlight just two of them. In order to become a certified coach through the ICF, you must attend a qualified coaching school to learn these competencies and then pass a test demonstrating your skills.

Active listening and powerful questioning are two essential qualities of effective coaches and leaders who want to operate in a more coach-like way to inspire and encourage their team to achieve their best efforts.

Active Listening

People may think that powerful coaching focuses on speaking and providing advice or solutions, but it actually starts with deep listening. Successful coaches have a way of listening that we call *committed listening*. It starts with listening from a commitment to "give people the gift of your presence,"—high-quality time and attention. It involves listening from a commitment to bring out the best in the person being coached. This new way of listening is not transactional in nature, giving advice or tips or using specific techniques. It embraces but goes beyond all this and is transformational with respect to the person being engaged with. Committed listening means listening from a commitment to the greatness (highest and best self) of the person being coached (the coachee) even when that person is not at his or her best.

It involves listening to understand what people passionately care about and how that links into the extraordinary future they want to create for themselves and their teams. Coaching creates a safe space for the person or team being coached to share deeply and fully when others are willing to listen deeply, with encouragement and without judgment.

Several of the skills ICF lists for active listening (http://www.coach federation.org/icfcredentials/core-competencies/) include:

- Hears the client's concerns, goals, values, and beliefs about what is and is not possible.
- Distinguishes between the words, the tone of voice, and the body language.
- Summarizes, paraphrases, reiterates, and mirrors back what client has said to ensure clarity and understanding.
- Encourages, accepts, explores, and reinforces the client's expression of feelings, perceptions, concerns, beliefs, suggestions, and so on.
- "Bottom-lines" or understands the essence of the client's communication and helps the client get there rather than engaging in long descriptive stories.

Powerful Questioning

My most impactful conversations, whether coaching or not, are in the first five minutes or less when you show up with presence and energy and powerful questions that shape the conversation into a deeper place. I ask myself how I can create the relationship with essence and energy to help the other person reveal more. The questions need to have meaning and context, which comes through listening and sincere connection.

—Sandy Scott, certified coach

There are many types of questions. Leading questions give the illusion that the other person is solving the problem, when in reality you are guiding that person to a definitive answer. Closed questions require limited choices such as "yes" or "no" and should be used infrequently. Coaching demands the use of powerful questioning.

The ICF definition of powerful questioning is the "ability to ask questions that reveal the information needed for maximum benefit to the coaching relationship and the client."

Some of the key skills ICF notes for powerful questioning include:

- Asks questions that reflect active listening and an understanding of the client's perspective.
- Asks questions that evoke discovery, insight, commitment, or action (e.g., those that challenge the client's assumptions).
- Asks open-ended questions that create greater clarity, possibility, or new learning.
- Asks questions that move the client towards what they desire, not questions that ask for the client to justify or look backwards.

Preparing to Be a Team Coach— Set Yourself Up for Success

As a team coach, your job is to work with the team leader and the team to help them achieve their goal. These games provide you with a fun way to engage the team in everything from icebreakers and relationship-building games to games that spur their creative thinking, improve their processes, and increase their ability to hold themselves accountable. Your mission, should you choose to accept it, is to find the right games and sequence them to achieve the desired results of that team. You are helping them move forward through the stages of team development into achieving an important goal for their organization. We wish you much success and fun on the journey.

2

The Benefits of Using Team Coaching Games

The path to greatness is along with others.

—Baltasar Gracián

People work most effectively when interacting with others they know and trust. Team coaching games, whether used with an intact work team, a project team, or an entire organization, enable people to build trust and rapport, which can lead to better outcomes. Team coaching games are versatile and can be used in a variety of situations:

- As a quick icebreaker to set a positive tone
- As the framework for a retreat
- At the beginning of a meeting
- To illustrate important points
- To reveal areas of potential concern
- To increase awareness of the team's strengths and opportunities
- To be a springboard for a deeper discussion
- To provide a metaphor or touchstone that the team can reflect upon
- To create a common language
- To provide a safe entry point to crucial conversations

If you think games are a waste of time, we encourage you to think deeper, reflect more, and open yourself to the idea that games provide more than meets the eye. Be open to the possibility that games can achieve a deeper level of connection with other team members and with the work to be done than meetings alone can accomplish.

The Benefits of Games

Listed below are the benefits of games.

Games Are Fun

When we are having fun, we have more energy; energy contributes to motivation, and with increased motivation, we are more productive. Playing games can revitalize a team and build morale.

Games Are Safe

Games provide a safe environment for individuals and teams to learn through trial and error. Mistakes and failure usually provide valuable lessons. Oftentimes, failure leads to something better—failure inspires creativity and innovation. Leadership may encourage teams to try new things; however, if those new things result in failure, there may be repercussions. In the context of games, team members can explore, take risks, try out new skills, and make mistakes without the threat of extreme consequences.

Games Reveal Team Dynamics

While playing games, the dynamics of the team are revealed. The coach and the team can examine the dynamics to ensure that they serve the team and will help the team achieve their goals. The team is able to consider its strengths and weaknesses. Through games, team members can observe how they navigate change, how they interact under stress, and what roles they take on in a variety of situations. These dynamics and more can be observed and processed in the safe environment of the game.

Games Build Self-Awareness and Awareness of Others

Just as the dynamics of the team can be examined, so can the individuals who make up the team. Through games, team members are given the opportunity to try new roles and to become aware of their function on the team and how they contribute to the team unit. Games also provide an opportunity to see team members in a new light. Hidden skills are uncovered and personalities shine, which can open up exciting new possibilities. The discussion allows time for reflection. Here, team members can build awareness by examining their own performance and contributions. The discussion is also a time for team members to recognize the contributions of others. The coach can provide team and individual analysis to build more self-awareness on the team.

Games Build Trust

The first step in building trust is creating an environment where team members can begin to build a deeper level of connection and comfort with one another. Games accelerate this process. The right games create opportunities for deeper levels of self-disclosure, which increases vulnerability; a willingness to be vulnerable lays the groundwork for trust.

Games Remind Team Members of the Value of the Team

Many of the games contain a component of competition versus collaboration. Even the word *game* incites the competitive spirit. When transferred to the workplace, competition leads to distrust and unwillingness to share information. Through playing games, team members become aware of the value of teamwork. They get to experience the results when a collaborative approach is taken.

Games Provide Learning Opportunities

Games are a wonderful learning tool. Each game provides lessons, skills, and experiences that team members learn by playing the game. Better problem solving, improved decision making, clearer communication, and more effective interpersonal interactions are examples of skills the team learns and practices while engaged in the game.

Games Foster Long-Term Retention

Because of the active-learning nature of games, teams not only learn more, but they retain the lesson longer. The high level of engagement carries through to the post-game discussion. The debriefing discussions provide a way to connect what team members learned and experienced to the way they get their work done on a typical day.

Getting the Most from the Games in This Book

Picking the Right Game

Using the right game at the right time is key. Before choosing a game, ask yourself a few questions, such as: "In what stage of group formation is the team? What are some issues the team needs to work through? What are some skills they need to practice or improve? What would stretch the team in new ways?" Once you have an idea of the reasoning behind using a game with the team, take a look at your options. At the start of each game, you will see a When to Use This Game recommendation. From there, take a look at the Objectives section to make sure the game is a good fit for the team at this point in its development. Another area to read is the Setting the Context section of the game. These three areas will give you a good idea whether the game is right for the team and whether the timing is right. To get the most from the games, using them in the right context at the right time will provide the best coaching opportunities for the team. One additional place to check is the time requirement. Team coaching games can create an environment for growth within the team when you allow time for team members to play the game as well as plenty of time to discuss how the game relates to the way they get their work done as a team.

Props and Prep

Two other areas to focus on before you begin are the Materials and Preparation sections. Most of these games require simple props. The Preparation section will provide tips on how you can prepare the setting for the best outcome. You may find it useful to keep some basic props on hand. Props that are frequently used in team coaching games include index cards, sticky notes, markers, masking tape, tennis balls, rope, flip-chart paper, and bandannas. Props such as these are all easy to compile and add an appealing feature to the games. After picking the best game to use with the team, get the handouts, flip charts, and props ready in advance to set yourself and the team up for success.

Do This First

Prior to coaching the team through any of these games, it's a good idea to convey the context for the activity—a framework to help the team see where the game fits into their development and provides value. Engage the team, provide the background, and share any necessary rules and guidelines. Then assign them their task, along with any time constraints. As team coach, you will be on high alert throughout the activity, taking notes, asking questions, and monitoring progress as the team undertakes their challenge. After the activity, take ample time for reflection and debriefing as this is where the team makes connections to the real world. You, or a team scribe, may want to document key ideas from the team discussion for next steps and follow-up.

Why Did We Do This? What Is the Message?
What Does It Mean for Us?

Games will remain games without an effectively facilitated debriefing discussion. Anticipate probable results and reactions, but at the same time be willing to allow team members to take the game where they take it. Take notes throughout the activity to refer to during the debriefing discussion. In addition to the discussion questions provided with the game's instructions, you may want to create other questions that are more tailored to suit the team or purpose. Asking the right questions will focus the team's attention on the meaning and purpose behind the game. You will find that many discussions develop organically after you prompt the team with one or two well-worded questions. Encourage team members to be responsible for generating meaningful conversation; consider starting the team discussion with a "pair and share" where two people discuss their experience and what applications it had for them. Don't be too quick to insert your own opinions and observations. Keep the discussion flowing, but also get comfortable with pauses as team members formulate their ideas and conclusions.

What Is the Connection?

All of the team coaching games in this book are intentionally broad in nature, so you can use them with any team, in any type of organization, within any industry. The coaching you provide throughout the game, the questions you ask, and your debriefing discussion can all be tailored to meet your objectives and the needs of the team. As the team coach, it's important that you allow team members to reflect on what happened in the game and the significance of what they experienced. How did the experience relate to them, their team dynamics, and their work?

Tips for Using Team Coaching Games

While many of these games can be played sitting or standing in a meeting, some of the games are more physical in nature and require some important guidelines. Following these commonsense tips will build trust between you, as the coach, and the team, and also ensure that your participants feel supported while they are stretching their comfort zones.

Follow the "challenge by choice" rule commonly used in experiential activities. Challenge by choice means every individual has the choice to participate at whatever level he or she feels comfortable. As coach, be sure to encourage team members to step out of their comfort zone and challenge themselves.

Set ground rules. These should be discussed and agreed upon by all participants. Examples of ground rules include: listen when others are speaking, ask questions, demonstrate support for others as they stretch their comfort zones, don't interrupt, show respect for the values of others, and so on.

Handle any potential safety issues. When using activities that require additional equipment, please make sure that the equipment is in good condition and is handled properly, and that individuals have the proper training and supervision necessary to perform the activity safely.

To make activities more challenging (particularly if you have group members who have done an activity before), consider instituting additional consequences or obstacles such as blindfolding, no talking, and mobility restrictions. If you choose to provide additional challenges for the team, such as blindfolding one team member, make sure that the individual is comfortable and willing to go this extra step. Nothing should be done at any time to intentionally place someone in a position they do not want to be in.

Be aware of rule violations. You can strictly enforce them or wait to see if the group regulates itself. Details like these can lead to robust discussions around ethics, values, and creativity.

Provide clear instructions, but do not get caught up in providing too much information. Answer questions and provide additional information when asked by the group. Some games rely on vague instructions to allow the team to interpret and act in any way they choose.

Use good judgment. It is important to provide the group with the proper balance of challenge and support so that team members stretch themselves and learn, but you don't want them to become overly frustrated and shut down.

Team Coaching and the Stages of Group Formation

The Forming Stage

This is the polite, get acquainted, and "get to know each other" stage. This is where team members begin to figure out who's who and where everyone fits into the picture. Typically, this takes place at the opening meeting or an orientation session and continues for a while as people get to know one another. A team goes through the stages of team formation again, when a new leader joins the team or several new team members are added to an existing team.

To get a head start on the forming stage, you can provide the team with each team member's qualifications and background information so everyone has an understanding of why the individuals were chosen for the team.

All the informal gatherings and discussions in and around the initial meeting are included in this stage of group formation for the intact team. The goal is to create an environment that is safe and secure. Because the team also looks for guidance and direction in the forming stage, the leader must ensure that the team's purpose is clearly communicated and understood by all team members. At this beginning stage, it's essential to get

buy-in from all the team members and candidly and honestly identify the pros and cons of teamwork and team building. This stage is where the team builds its foundation, so time spent in this stage will pay off later.

Forming may last for a short time or take several months for the team to move through. A team coach can assist the team leader with the methodologies to enhance success. For the reader who is familiar with *Self Leadership and the One Minute Manager: Increasing Effectiveness Through Situational Self Leadership,* we offer the suggestions of authors Ken Blanchard, Susan Fowler, and Laurence Hawkins as they tie each phase of situational leadership to the stages of group formation. In the forming stage, the role of the leader and team coach is to provide direction. The games found in Chapter 3 are helpful during the forming stage.

The Storming Stage

In this stage, interpersonal issues often arise. This stage is typically where conflict gets introduced into a previously safe and comfortable environment. There may be fear and uncertainty of change or of status loss, as well as lack of trust when the motivations for others' actions are not understood, yet there is not enough trust to have open dialogue about the problem. These conflicts provide team members with opportunities to learn how to interact effectively with one another. Storming takes place when things that may not have mattered in the beginning suddenly seem important and conflict ensues. You may experience this stage starting at week two, three, or four, or even later. This will depend on the frequency of communication within the team, and how much trust and camaraderie was developed in the forming stage.

This stage can be extremely frustrating. Some teams never make it out of this challenging stage. While face-to-face communication allows for immediate feedback and provides nonverbal cues, the team may struggle with this stage and become frustrated by the amount of time it takes to resolve conflict and learn the best ways to communicate with other team members. Team members will look to the leader and coach to support them as they navigate through this stormy stage.

Many issues can cause separation on a team. To ensure that unforeseen issues don't arise to fracture the team, develop protocols for using various types of technology for communication, along with training to ensure that all team members are comfortable and willing to use the best communication method for the situation. For example, the use of email as a sole communication method hinders a team's ability to navigate through conflict. Know when to use face-to-face meetings, the phone, webcams, and so on to talk through more challenging situations to minimize miscommunication. Use the game Gravity Stick (page 175) to give the team a chance to practice conflict resolution and also to open the door to a team discussion about conflict. It is critical that these concerns be dealt with honestly. When interpersonal conflicts and dissonance are handled at this early stage, the team has a better chance of success.

Once again, leadership will be necessary to navigate through the storming stage, so the leader or team coach should facilitate games that help the team to work through the natural storming process. The leader should also lead discussions to ensure the team can use the appropriate tools when interacting with each other day to day. In the storming stage, the role of the leader and team coach is to provide support and direction and to provide reinforcement of ideas, skills, and accountability check-ins to keep the team focused and future oriented.

The Norming Stage

Cooperation and trust are now becoming the "norm" for this team. Team members begin to better understand one another's diverse personalities and work styles, enabling them to work together more effectively. Team members should also have a handle on which communication methods are preferred and most efficient when interacting with other team members.

Good things are starting to happen, and as a result, the team feels more confident, connected, and creative. In the norming stage, the role of the leader and team coach is to provide support when team members take on new challenges, to ask questions to open up new possibilities, and to continue to hold team members accountable for achieving results and working collaboratively.

Many of the games in this book are suitable for teams that have reached this stage and are open to sharing honestly with one another in order to enable the team to move toward reaching the performing stage.

The Performing Stage

Here, the team is highly effective. The team has momentum and energy and ideally all team members are willing to contribute their best efforts. The performing stage is the most productive of all the stages. "Performing" indicates that team members have a clear, shared sense of purpose, high trust, and open communication. Team spirit is high, relationships are improved, and there is a strong feeling of camaraderie. Tasks are identified and handled efficiently by the members of the team. Individuals respect the contributions of others, and the team is well on its way to meeting, and even surpassing, its goals and objectives—all the while maintaining a sense of unity and cohesion. In addition, the stress involved with deadlines, transitions, and changes can influence the way team members communicate. Incorporating a game such as Go (page 149) or Team Story Time Line (page 183) can be beneficial in the performing stage. Team members have a chance to check in with one another and be heard by the team. Remember that conflict on a team is normal, and by now your team should have some experience with and confidence in handling conflict. As leader, you can help to mitigate and direct that conflict in a positive and constructive manner. Remember, if everyone always agrees, you may not be hearing honest input and great ideas may be squelched. In the performing stage, the role of the leader and team coach is to ask questions to allow for reflection and new possibilities and to work with the team to set new and more challenging goals.

The Transforming Stage

The transforming stage brings closure. Transforming occurs when the team is at such an effective level of functioning that it can redefine its shared purpose and respond quickly to change. The leadership within the team is shared, trust is high, and communication is open. The team you have in this stage is a far different team than the one you started with. Developing a successful team takes time, patience, and a willingness to develop both the relationships and process for successfully achieving goals. The relationships established on a successful team are well established and may continue long after the team disbands. Make sure you allow time for closure and reflection. As a leader or a coach, be ready with plenty of recognition, appreciation, and celebration. Give team members ample time to recognize and appreciate each other, as well as their hard-earned success. Kudos to You (page 197) is an excellent game for team members to provide specific recognition to others.

What to Expect

Normally, each stage of team development takes several months to move forward. Teams that interact more frequently and deliberately will move more quickly through the stages. Conversely, teams that interact infrequently and less purposefully may take much longer to progress through the stages. A team leader who understands the stages can help a team navigate the stages in a healthier and more productive manner. Getting to the performing and transforming stages can take as long as two years, based on the research of Bruce Tuckman, founder of this model of group formation.

Using an experienced, capable team coach with a specific process and using the team coaching games in this book can vastly impact the learning and performance of team members to move through the stages and reach their stride much more quickly.

Why Do the Stages Matter?

First, it can be helpful to know that there are stages and that it is normal for all teams to go through these stages. Second, it enables the leader and team coach to identify the stage of development for a given group or team and assist the movement through that stage by managing the communication, visioning, and other dynamics among team members. If there is low trust, the leader and team coach can deploy trust-building exercises. If the team is unclear or not in alignment about its purpose, there are games and techniques to focus on to help determine the team's collective priorities. Assessing the stage a team is in can provide insight into which game will provide the right amount of challenge, which game will allow for the greatest growth opportunity, and which game will have the greatest impact on the team.

3

Meeting the Players

Individually, we are one drop. Together, we are an ocean.

—Ryunosuke Satoro

Accents Are Fun

WHEN TO USE THIS GAME

As an icebreaker or "get to know you better" activity

OBJECTIVES
- To get to know more about other team members
- To have fun while focusing on team members' diverse backgrounds or experiences

Group Size

Any

Materials

None

Time

15 to 20 minutes

Setting the Context

People's accents sound interesting when they are from "someplace else." Teams often represent a cross section of people who were raised in different parts of the United States and possibly from all over the world. Accents can also be a source of frustration as we don't always understand what the other person is saying. As we interact with others, it is important to focus on the positives of our diversity. This is a fun activity to get people to realize that we all have unique backgrounds that contribute to our overall success.

Preparation

None

Procedure

Tell the team that, in order for team members to get to know each other a bit better, each person will share a favorite story from his or her child-hood. To make it more interesting, each person should use an exaggerated accent or dialect of the people in the region he or she is from, or perhaps of an elderly relative who immigrated from another country. Whether people are from New England, the South, or "across the pond," the regional accents make us realize the richness of our interwoven team.

Rules

- Everyone participates.
- If people say they are not good at accents, just ask them to give it their best shot.

Discussion Questions

1. What did you enjoy about this activity?

2. How does this help increase awareness of the rich diversity of your team?

3. How can you give your work a light, fun component?

Coach Note: As a variation, especially if many team members are from the same area, you might change the activity to ask each person to share a story of a favorite travel destination or favorite vacation spot and use the accent or key words that are used in that destination.

Animal Magnetism

WHEN TO USE THIS GAME

As a check-in tool to see how people are feeling

OBJECTIVES

- To see what emotions are on or under the surface
- To recognize that people bring emotions and feelings to work

Group Size

Any

Materials

Pictures of wild and domestic animals
(2 to 3 per person)

Time

5 minutes to set up and about 2 minutes per person

Setting the Context

In the workplace, we often act as if emotions and feelings don't exist. The goal of this game is to become more comfortable talking about these areas. If team members can honestly express their positive and negative emotions in a safe way, they are better able to bond and support one another.

Preparation

Arrange the pictures on a table.

Procedure

Invite individuals to come and choose a picture that depicts how they are currently feeling.

Rules

- Choose a picture that best describes how you are currently feeling.
- If none of the pictures feels right, you can draw a picture or use your phone to search the Internet for another image.

Discussion Questions

1. What did you learn about your team?
2. How does it feel to share at a deeper level?
3. Why does it sometimes feel taboo to talk about feelings and stress in the workplace?
4. How can you support one another?

Coach Note: After each person shares, you could do a second round where individuals choose the animal they feel like when they are at their best and describe why. Allow additional time.

Know Thyself

WHEN TO USE THIS GAME
To increase self-awareness and have team members get to know each other better

OBJECTIVES
- To dig deeper into what helps you to be your best
- To reflect and deepen self-awareness

Group Size
Any

Materials
Colored construction paper, crayons or markers, music

Time
30 to 60 minutes depending on group size

Setting the Context
This is a great activity for team members who are just getting to know one another as well as those who already know each other well. It enables a deeper conversation to occur about what brings out the best in each person as well as what does not, and what steps people can take as a team to show their best selves.

Preparation
Have supplies available and table space to work at.

Procedure
Tell the team that this is an exercise to really get to know one another better and to dig deeper into self-awareness. Ask them to think about a time when they were "at their best." You might ask, "What did you feel like?" "What were you doing?" "How were you interacting with others?"

Now ask them to think about a time when they were *not* "at their best." (**Coach Note:** Do not say, "When you were at your worst.") You might ask, "What did you feel like?" "What were you doing?" "How were you interacting with others?"

Say, "Now that you have both of those images in your mind, I'd like you to select a piece of construction paper and use one side to draw a picture of yourself when you are at your best and the other side to draw a representation of when you are not at your best." Encourage them, saying that artistic talent is not as important as having fun with this exercise and sharing honestly. Stick figures are just fine.

Tell them, "You will have fifteen minutes. I will let you know when you have ten, then five minutes remaining. You will be sharing these pictures with the team."

You may want to play background music while the team works to enhance the creative process. While they are working, walk around the room and offer support and encouragement. At the appointed time, see if they are ready. They may need a few more minutes. One at a time, until everyone has shared, ask for volunteers to share their pictures and describe themselves in the two scenarios.

Rules
- Everyone creates two pictures, one depicting when they are at their best and one depicting when they are not at their best.
- Everyone shares both pictures.

Discussion Questions
1. What did you learn about yourself?
2. What did you learn about the team?
3. How can you help each other be your best selves more often?
4. What barriers might need to be removed? What habits could be changed?
5. How do you create an environment where you can ask for what you need?

Life Map

WHEN TO USE THIS GAME
Early in your team's development to begin connecting the team members to one another on a deeper level

OBJECTIVES
- To build trust
- To gain a deeper understanding of others on the team

Group Size
Any

Materials
Paper, colored markers and pens

Time
30 to 40 minutes

Setting the Context
Don't be fooled by this seemingly innocuous activity—it can be the catalyst to developing a greater level of trust within the team. Trust is developed when individuals open up about themselves on a personal level. This takes a willingness to be vulnerable, so as team coach, make sure you provide the right amount of support and encouragement during this activity.

Preparation
None

Procedure
Pass out one piece of paper to each team member. Make several different colored markers and pens available for them to use for their drawings. Ask team members to draw a map of their life, including whatever experiences, events, places, and people contributed to their life story. Tell them they will have exactly ten minutes to create their life map. At the end of ten minutes,

go around the team and invite each person to share their life map and the story that goes along with it.

Coach Notes: This activity is quiet and reflective, yet can be very powerful. When given the right framework, it allows people to open up and share in a way they might not otherwise do. This activity tends to create a warm and accepting atmosphere. You will hear in-depth stories and significant life experiences. As coach, be prepared to ask and encourage follow-up questions. In addition, be sure to lead the celebration as significant life events are shared to foster a supportive, celebratory culture in your team.

Silent Interview

WHEN TO USE THIS GAME

As team members are getting to know each other

OBJECTIVES

- To build awareness of nonverbal messages
- To get to know other team members better

Group Size

Up to 20, paired up with partners

Materials

None

Time

10 to 20 minutes

Setting the Context

Nonverbal communication is a large component of our everyday interactions. An effective coach not only listens to what is said but also has a high level of awareness as to what is being conveyed through body language. The more we know someone else, the easier it is to determine what that person is telling us nonverbally. As coaches, we want to make sure our interpretations are accurate and to be able to check our interpretations in a nonthreatening manner. Using a game like this builds awareness that our interpretations may not always be correct, and that we should check for accuracy rather than assume understanding.

Preparation

None

Procedure

Ask the team what nonverbal communication consists of. Gain agreement that nonverbal communication does not involve any talking, mouthing words, or whispering. Tell team members that this short activity relies solely on nonverbal communication and ask their permission to hold them accountable to the nonverbal standards they came up with. Once you have agreement, you are ready to begin the game.

Procedure

- Have team members form partnerships with others who they don't know very well. For well-established teams who all know each other, ask team members to partner with the person they have the least daily contact with.
- Ask the participants to greet each other with a handshake.
- Instruct the team that from this point forward, only nonverbal communication is allowed.
- Tell the participants that they must convey to their partner three things about themselves without speaking. Challenge them to go beyond physical characteristics, such as being tall or short, wearing glasses, or having a butterfly tattoo.
- Partners can check their understanding if they choose; however, this must be done nonverbally as well.
- Once all of the partners have finished "talking" to each other, gather everyone back together.
- Ask each pair to present the three things that they learned or think they learned about each other.
- Allow time for laughter and clarification.

Discussion Questions

1. How accurate were your interpretations overall?
2. How much of your daily interactions with each other are nonverbal? What are some examples?
3. How can you check for understanding?
4. What are some questions you can ask to clarify understanding?
5. When your nonverbal communication is sending a negative message and impacting team performance, would you like to be coached? What is the best way to do that?

The Weather Is...

OBJECTIVES

- To warm the team up to sharing feelings
- To quickly capture the mood of the team

Group Size

Any

Materials

None; or can use construction paper and colored pens or markers

Time

10 to 25 minutes, depending on group size and variation

Setting the Context

This is a quick, safe way for people to express how they are feeling.

Preparation

Have supplies on hand if you want to use them.

Procedure

If you want to use this as a quick check-in, you could say, "We're all familiar with the daily weather report. Outside, today's weather forecast is...[share local forecast or best guess]."

Say, "Take a minute now to reflect on how you are feeling. How present are you? How is your health? What is your current energy level? You will have fifteen seconds to state your current status like a weather report. For example, 'I feel partly sunny but see a few clouds on the horizon.'" Give the group a minute to reflect on what they want to say. Ask for a volunteer, then proceed to have everyone share. If this precedes a challenging conversation, you may wish to check in after the conversation as well, to see how "their weather forecast" has changed.

Rule
- Everyone shares.

Discussion Questions
1. How did it feel to share your feelings or current status in this way?

2. How does your personal weather forecast impact those around you?

3. What can help you change the weather forecast?

Variations
If you want to tap into team members' creativity as well as their emotional/energy state, ask them to draw a picture of how they are feeling. Allow five to ten minutes for drawing, then proceed to share as above. You may choose to post the pictures.

Thumb Ball

WHEN TO USE THIS GAME

Anytime, to help team members build and strengthen their working relationships with each other.

> **OBJECTIVES**
> - To develop trust among and learn more about fellow team members
> - To understand the attitudes, backgrounds, and beliefs of fellow team members

Group Size
6 to 20

Materials
Permanent marker, one beach ball or lightweight soccer ball, Thumb Ball Questions handout

Time
10 to 15 minutes

Setting the Context

Trust among group members is essential for a healthy, well-functioning team. This exercise gives team members a chance to build trust as they share some personal fun facts, career-related stories, and beliefs and attitudes about work and leadership.

Preparation

Using a permanent marker, write the numbers 1 through 32 randomly all around the surface of a beach ball or soccer ball. Copy the Thumb Ball Questions handout.

Procedure

Have the group stand in a circle. Tell them that they will be tossing the Thumb Ball from one person to the next, and that team members will answer a question when the ball comes to them. Some of the questions will be work related, while others will be fun facts about them that their teammates might not know. Use soft underhand tosses for this activity.

The team coach will select someone across the circle from him or her and toss that person the Thumb Ball. He or she should read aloud the number located under his or her right thumb. Read the corresponding question from the Thumb Ball Questions handout. If the question has already been asked, have the person announce the number under his or her left thumb. If participants do not wish to answer a question, they can choose to toss the ball up in the air and catch it themselves in order to get another question.

After a person answers a question, he or she should toss the ball to someone new so that everyone gets a chance to play.

Variations

Create your own list of Thumb Ball Questions to match the needs of your group. If team members are just getting to know each other, include questions that are light, fun, and easy to answer. If team members have lots of experience together, include questions that probe a bit more deeply into their attitudes about leadership, ethics, career success, or other relevant topics.

Thumb Ball Questions

1. Who is a person you admire?

2. What is your ideal vacation?

3. What is a board game you enjoy?

4. What is a nonwork activity you enjoy?

5. Who makes you laugh?

6. What is the most recent book you've read, or are currently reading?

7. What is a favorite toy from your childhood?

8. What are two office tools you can't live without?

9. What project are you most proud of?

10. What business are you a loyal customer of?

11. What is an important thing that happened recently at work?

12. What helps keep you organized?

13. What is an event you would like to witness if you had a time machine?

14. What are two valuable traits in a coworker?

15. What advice would you give to someone starting his or her career?

16. What was your first job?

17. What are some pros and cons of being a leader?

18. What was your smartest career decision?

19. What is an unusual profession you would be willing to try?

20. What are two practical skills you possess?

21. How does the Internet best serve you?

22. What are two ways to stay motivated or inspired?

23. What is an item you never travel without?

24. What is the name of your favorite pet?

25. What risk have you taken recently?

26. What sports championship do you enjoy watching most?

27. What TV show makes you laugh?

28. If you were to write a book, what would it be about?

29. What movie or TV show has inspired you?

30. What is something you consider yourself an authority on?

31. Who do you consider a great actor or actress?

32. What is a favorite book from your childhood?

Where My Strength Comes From

WHEN TO USE THIS GAME
To get to know each other better

OBJECTIVES
- To learn more about each other
- To respect the differences between the team members

Group Size
Any

Materials
One piece of paper and one pen for each person (may need additional paper and markers); personal items that participants provide; one or more large boxes or paper bags to store items

Time
30 to 45 minutes

Setting the Context

Everyone draws their strength from somewhere. For Popeye, it was a can of spinach; for some it's running; for others it may be playing with their children. This activity helps the team learn more about what it is that recharges and strengthens the emotional and energetic batteries of their peers. It's a fun way to get to know more about each other and perhaps find some common bonds.

Preparation

Ask each person ahead of time to bring one item that symbolizes something that centers them, energizes them, or brings them comfort or strength. (**Hint:** Ask them at least a week in advance and then remind them the day before the event.) They are not to share what this item is with anyone else in advance. As people arrive, put the items into a large box or paper bag so they remain hidden from view. Lay out pens and pieces of paper around the tables, leaving enough space to add one item by each piece of paper. Have the tables spread around the room, if possible, to encourage circulation. You may want to ask someone to help lay out all of the items.

Procedure

Invite everyone to look over all of the items and then to write down the name of the person who they think brought the item on the piece of paper next to it. Allow about ten to fifteen minutes, depending on the number of people and items. Encourage them to guess—there is no penalty for being wrong.

When everyone has written down their guess for each item, invite the group to be seated. Ask for volunteers to come up and claim their item one at a time. Ask them to share why they chose it and how it represents where their strength comes from or how they stay centered. After they share, ask them to look at the list and see how many people guessed correctly that this was their item. Continue until everyone has shared.

Rules

- Everyone needs to bring an item. If they do not, have them draw an item before the activity begins or download a picture from the Internet.
- If they are unable to do any of the above, just have them share at the end what they would have chosen and why it has meaning.

Discussion Questions

1. What common themes did you notice?
2. What surprised you?
3. How can you help each other turn to your strengths during challenging times?

Coach Note: You could choose to offer a prize for the person who was guessed correctly most often and/or for the one(s) guessed least correctly.

Work Styles

WHEN TO USE THIS GAME

Early on, to provide insight into the preferences and personalities of others on the team

OBJECTIVES

- To discover our own and others' preferred work styles
- To increase team members' ability to be "other" focused

Group Size

Up to 20, split into teams of 4 to 5

Materials

Yellow, Orange, Blue, and Green Game Cards cutouts; Working Together with Different Styles handout; pens or pencils

Time

30 to 40 minutes

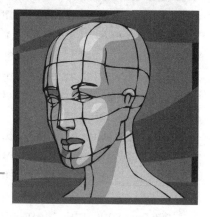

Setting the Context

Building trust requires a willingness to break down some barriers and let others get to know us better: our personalities, our preferences, our strengths, and our weaknesses. This is a high-energy and interactive approach to assessing the members of the team. Who are the players? After this game, participants will know each other, and maybe even themselves, a little better.

Preparation

Copy and cut out the cards provided, making sure to copy each style on the cardstock indicated on each card template. One set of cards will supply enough for a team of up to twenty people.

Procedure

Split your group into small teams of four to five people. Shuffle all the cards so there is a mixture of different colors to pass around.

Step one: Pass out five cards (facedown) to each person. When everyone has five cards, invite team members to turn over their cards and put them in order from most to least descriptive of their personality. Once the cards are ordered, participants explain to their team why they put their cards in the order they did.

Step two: Now they can trade cards with anyone on their small team; the goal is to get a hand that reflects their personality more accurately. After the trading, ask everyone to discard two cards, keeping the three cards that reflect their personality most accurately.

Step three: Next, open the trading to the entire group—again the goal is to get the best (most accurate) hand.

Step four: After a few minutes of whole-room trading, allow trading with any of the discarded cards (which have been placed faceup on tables around the room).

Step five: Participants end up with three cards each. Have them once again prioritize the cards. If they have two or three of the same color, then that's their style. If they have three different colors, the top colored card is their style.

Once everyone understands their final color, have them group together with others of the same color. After they are grouped together and standing with others of their style, and before sitting down to answer the Working Together with Different Styles handout, have them read aloud the three cards they ended up with.

Give each of the four work-style teams a handout and have participants answer the questions together. Once the teams are finished, gather for a group discussion.

Discussion Questions

1. How does this allow you to better understand yourself and others on the team?

2. In what ways does this benefit the team?

3. How can team members continue to gain a deeper level of understanding of each other?

4. What important team skills are uncovered with an activity such as this?

5. How can you develop these skills as you work together?

Yellow Game Cards

(Copy on yellow cardstock.)

Bold	Risk-taker
Intense	Gets it done
Productive	Natural leader
Likes control	Goal-oriented
Confident	Decisive
Daring	Restless
Competitive	Assertive
Forceful	Determined
Strong-willed	Impatient
Direct	Independent
Powerful	Opinionated
Challenging	Manages time
Succinct	Human bulldozer
Can't stand inactivity	Demanding of self
Straightforward	Gets point across
Results-driven	Self-assured
Organized	Fast-paced

Orange Game Cards

(Copy on orange cardstock.)

Optimistic	Enthusiastic
Open	Impulsive
Emotional	Talkative
Charming	Adventurous
Trusting	Spirited
Charismatic	Positive
Fun-loving	Engaging
Spontaneous	Energetic
Animated	Sociable
Warm and genuine	Likeable
Idea-centered	Open to contributing
Flexible	Cheerful
Curious	Loves people
Expressive	Motivating
Demonstrative	Inspires others
Loves the spotlight	Influencing
Persuasive	Convincing

Blue Game Cards

(Copy on blue cardstock.)

Willing	Conforming
Objective	Agreeable
Harmonious	Tolerant
Caring	Good listener
Likes collaborative efforts	Amiable
Accepting	Interested
Deliberate	Predictable
Patient	Accommodating
Easygoing	Cooperative
Supportive	Dislikes confrontation
Adaptable	Indecisive
Even-tempered	Content
Sensitive	Cool and collected
Competent	Mediates problems
Calm	Lenient
Empathetic	Steady
Natural team player	Helpful

Green Game Cards

(Copy on green cardstock.)

Cautious	Logical
Analytical	Precise
Skeptical	Tactful
Consistent	Perfectionist
Detail-oriented	Factual
Exacting	Likes rules
Accurate	Reserved
Disciplined	Self-critical
Conservative	Focused
Likes data	Private
Industrious	Structured
Quality-centered	Natural planner
Serious	Purposeful
Sees the problems	Economical
Follows through	Thorough
Does it right	High standards
Resourceful	Careful

Working Together with Different Styles

Please discuss these questions with your team and come to a consensus. So that team members grouped in other styles get a good working knowledge of what your style is all about, provide a thorough answer for each question.

At work and being part of a team . . .

- Who are we when we're at our best?

- What skills and qualities do we bring to the team?

- How do we typically prefer to give feedback?

- How do we prefer to receive feedback?

- How to we prefer to accomplish tasks?

- How do we like to be held accountable?

- How do we like to be recognized for a job well done?

Building a Positive Team Culture

A player who makes a team great is more valuable than a great player.

—John Wooden

Blindfold Trust Walk

WHEN TO USE THIS GAME

When you recognize that the team needs a deeper level of trust

OBJECTIVES

- To build trust and supportive relationships among team members
- To improve communication

Group Size

Any, paired up with partners

Materials

One blindfold for each person (optional)

Time

25 to 30 minutes

Setting the Context

In his book *The Five Dysfunctions of a Team,*
Patrick Lencioni describes trust as the basis for
all effective teamwork: "Trust lies at the heart of a functioning, cohesive
team. Without it, teamwork is all but impossible"[1] As a coach, one of your
top priorities must be to help the team build a spirit of trust and mutual
interdependence. This classic exercise gives team members a chance to
experience trust in action and to explore issues related to feedback, trust-
worthiness, and communication.

Preparation

Find a location with plenty of space for two people to walk side by side. It
can be indoors, outdoors, or both. Because team members will be taking
turns wearing blindfolds or closing their eyes, choose an area with mini-
mal tripping hazards or unsafe obstacles.

---

1 Patrick Lencioni, *The Five Disfunctions of a Team* (San Francisco: Jossey-Bass, 2002), 195.

Procedure

Begin by inviting team members to form groups of two. If there is an extra person left over, have that person join one of the groups to make a trio. Tell them that they will be taking a walk together, with one partner wearing a blindfold or closing his or her eyes and the other partner being the "blind" partner's sighted guide.

The guide's job is to take his or her "blind" partner on a walk for ten minutes. They may go anywhere the guide chooses, as long as the area is safe and free of hazards. During the walk, guides will communicate verbally with their partners to keep them on a safe path and steer them clear of obstacles. Encourage guides to use positive communication and be aware of the needs of their unsighted partners along the way.

After ten minutes, have the partners stop. Ask the original "blind" partners to provide some feedback to their guides. Have them share what they felt their guide did that was good, as well as offer suggestions that could help them do even better.

When they are done providing feedback, invite the partners to switch roles. As before, give everyone ten minutes for their walk, followed by a short debriefing session with their partner.

Discussion Questions

1. What was it like being in the role of guide?

2. What was it like being in the role of the unsighted partner?

3. What did your guide do to make you feel safe and comfortable?

4. Did anyone experience something that resulted in a loss of trust?

5. Was feedback requested and shared effectively?

6. What are some warning signs that might indicate a lack of trust on a team?

7. What are some signs that indicate a team has a high level of trust?

8. What are some real-life ways that a team can build trust?

Debate Versus Dialogue

WHEN TO USE THIS GAME
When team members advocate for their position without considering others' perspectives

OBJECTIVES
- To understand the difference between debate and dialogue
- To develop the dialogue skills of team members

Group Size
Up to 20

Materials
Debate Versus Dialogue Game Cards cutout and handout

Time
20 to 30 minutes

Setting the Context
The minute we think someone else may be of a different opinion, a competitive instinct takes over and we dig our heels in and defend our position. Listening is nonexistent, because as the other person is talking we are debunking what he or she has to say and formulating our talking points to prove our point when it's our turn to talk again. Or we silently seethe, unwilling to voice our opinions due to a lack of trust. Once team members are introduced to the distinction between debate and dialogue, it opens their minds to the possibility of the "both, and" approach, rather than the "either, or" approach.

Preparation
Copy and cut out one set of the Debate Versus Dialogue Game Cards.

Procedure

Say to the team: "We are going to play a game called Debate Versus Dialogue. In a minute I will pass out twenty cards facedown so you each have approximately the same number of cards. On each card is a trait of either debate or dialogue, and each card has a partner card. For example, your card may say, 'Winning is the end goal.' The partner card may say, 'Discovering the best solution is the end goal.' Your task is to match up the partner cards and place them next to each other on the table."

Pass out the cards and read these rules to your team:

Rules

- You can only look at your own cards.
- You may share the information on your cards verbally, but no one else can look at your cards.
- Your task is to find your partner card by interacting with others to discover which cards match up the best.
- When you find the partner card to your card, place them faceup next to each other on the table.
- Once a card is on the table, it cannot be moved or rearranged.
- When all cards are on the table, review them as a team to ensure the cards are matched in the manner that makes the most sense.
- After all the cards are on the table, give the team the Debate Versus Dialogue Answers handout to check their answers.

Variations

For teams with fewer than eight members, place the cards faceup on a table and have the whole team match up the cards together.

Discussion Questions

1. What are the benefits of dialogue?
2. When is dialogue most appropriate?
3. What are the challenges of engaging in dialogue?
4. What team norms can be created to foster dialogue skills?
5. How would you like to be held accountable?
6. How can you hold each other accountable?

Debate Versus Dialogue Game Cards

Debate	Dialogue
Assuming that there is a right answer, and you have it	Assuming that many people have pieces of the answer
Combative: participants attempt to prove the other side wrong	Collaborative: participants work together toward common understanding
About winning	About exploring common ground
Listening to find flaws and make counterarguments	Listening to understand, find meaning and agreement
Defending our own assumptions as truth	Revealing our assumptions for reevaluation
Seeing two sides of an issue	Seeing all sides of an issue
Defending one's own views against those of others	Admitting that others' thinking can improve on one's own
Searching for flaws and weaknesses in others' positions	Searching for strengths and value in others' positions
By creating a winner and a loser, discouraging further discussion	Keeping the topic open even after the discussion formally ends
Seeking a conclusion or vote that ratifies your position	Discovering new options, not seeking closure

Debate Versus Dialogue Answers

Debate	Dialogue
Assuming that there is a right answer, and you have it	Assuming that many people have pieces of the answer
Combative: participants attempt to prove the other side wrong	Collaborative: participants work together toward common understanding
About winning	About exploring common ground
Listening to find flaws and make counterarguments	Listening to understand, find meaning and agreement
Defending our own assumptions as truth	Revealing our assumptions for reevaluation
Seeing two sides of an issue	Seeing all sides of an issue
Defending one's own views against those of others	Admitting that others' thinking can improve on one's own
Searching for flaws and weaknesses in others' positions	Searching for strengths and value in others' positions
By creating a winner and a loser, discouraging further discussion	Keeping the topic open even after the discussion formally ends
Seeking a conclusion or vote that ratifies your position	Discovering new options, not seeking closure

Source: Gerzon (2006).

Feetza, Feetza!

WHEN TO USE THIS GAME

Anytime to energize and challenge the group

OBJECTIVES

- To experience a fun, creative problem-solving challenge
- To energize the team and engage in some light, friendly competition

Group Size

At least 8

Materials

Tape measure

Time

15 minutes

Setting the Context

Sometimes nothing brings a team together better than sharing some laughs! This creative problem-solving challenge is lots of fun and a great way to energize the team, especially after a long or serious meeting. It's inspired by Karl Rohnke's Leaning Tower of Feetza game, found in his book *Funn 'n Games*.

Preparation

None

Procedure

Split the group into two or more competing teams of between four and fifteen people. (Bigger teams are more fun for this activity.) Tell the teams they will be competing to create the tallest freestanding tower possible, using only their shoes as building materials. Allow ten minutes for the teams to build their towers and five minutes to measure them to determine the tallest tower.

Rules

- Only shoes may be used in the towers. Shoelaces, tassels, and buckles are all okay to use, as long as they are a part of someone's shoes.
- Towers may not lean against walls, chairs, or any other external means of support.
- People may not use their hands or any part of their bodies to support their tower.

Discussion Questions

1. How did your team approach this challenge?

2. What roles did people play?

3. What can your team do to encourage creative problem solving at work?

Funny Face

WHEN TO USE THIS GAME

To open a discussion around the skill of nonjudgmental listening in a lighthearted, fun way

OBJECTIVES
- To foster engagement
- To discuss the implications of apathy

Group Size

Any

Materials

One large paper grocery bag for each person, colored markers, several nonfiction or reference books or journals (such as dictionaries, technical manuals, instruction manuals, law journals, or medical journals)

Time

20 minutes

Setting the Context

Listening in a nonjudgmental manner is a high-level coaching skill that any team member can learn to use to help coach their fellow teammates. This activity allows the team to recognize the difference between being nonjudgmental and apathetic. It provides a place for team members to discuss the skills involved in listening and how team members can support each other as they practice those skills. It also provides an opening for a discussion about apathy and its impact on a team.

Preparation

The coach needs to prepare an example bag as described on the next page.

Procedure

Give each team member one paper grocery bag and invite each participant to draw a funny face on the front of his or her bag. It's a good idea to have one example bag on display with a large, colorful, and exaggerated funny face drawn on the front. Tell the team to draw a face large enough so that if the bag were put on a person's head, other participants could easily see the face from across the room.

Ask the team what skills are required to listen effectively. Ask them to clarify what it means to listen nonjudgmentally. What stops us from doing this? What are the benefits for the other person when we listen without judging? How does this contribute to a culture of coaching?

Next ask the group to clarify the difference between being nonjudgmental and apathetic. Discuss with the group what apathy is. What does it mean? What causes apathy?

Then explain to the group that they are going to practice being apathetic. Have team members take turns reading from one of the books or journals. They must show total apathy at all times, which means using no facial expressions and reading in a monotonous voice. The other team members must also be completely apathetic as they listen to each person read. If anyone shows any emotion other than complete apathy, any team member may call out, "I accuse thee of expressiveness," using complete apathy, as he or she points to the guilty team member. The expressive team member must then put the bag over his or her head until that person has stopped showing expression.

You will soon find that this turns into a total laughfest, with team members having to keep bags over their heads for a significant period of time.

Discussion Questions

1. What is the difference between being nonjudgmental and apathetic?
2. How can you tell when another person is apathetic?
3. In what ways does an apathetic team member impact the team?
4. Have you ever been apathetic? What caused this? How did you reengage?
5. Now let's discuss nonjudgmental listening; how can you tell if you are being listened to in this manner?
6. How does it help the team to incorporate this skill?
7. How can the team support you as you practice nonjudgmental listening?

Grumble, Whine, and Complain

WHEN TO USE THIS GAME
Early in the team's inception to introduce and role-play the idea
of reframing negatives into positives

OBJECTIVES
- To consider the upside in seemingly negative situations
- To build the confidence of team members

Group Size

Any, paired up with partners

Materials

Paper and pens, stopwatch

Time

20 to 30 minutes

Setting the Context
A healthy team easily listens to one
another and provides helpful feedback. Team members listen to the emotions behind the words spoken, ask questions, and help each other see the
upside of failure and setbacks.

Preparation
You will need a space large enough so everyone can take their chairs in
pairs and spread out to talk without disrupting other partnerships.

Procedure
Have team members find a partner. Provide each pair with paper and pens.
Invite partners to find a place where they can sit and have a quiet conver-
sation with limited distractions.

This activity consists of two stages. Explain stage one like this:

"The first thing you need to do is figure out which partner is person A and which partner is person B. [Pause while they do this.] For the next two minutes, person A will be complaining to person B about whatever he or she chooses to complain about. Person B, your job is to simply listen while person A complains. Your job is not to fix, suggest, or provide any solutions. Most importantly, your job is not to say something like, 'You think you have it bad, here's what happened to me….' The first two minutes are all about person A and his or her gripes."

As the game leader, you can stop them after one minute and say, "That was only one minute; did you have enough time?" One minute is usually a sufficient amount of time to air grievances. After you call time, instruct person B to jot down some notes as a reminder of what he or she heard. Allow another minute for this step. When you get the sense that most are finished, ask them to set their notes aside.

Now it is person B's turn to complain to person A. Allow one minute for complaining, followed by another minute for person A to jot down notes about what he or she heard. The first part of your debriefing consists of the partners sharing with each other the manner in which they reframed their partner's complaints. Allow plenty of time for the partners to share and discuss their observations as complainer and listener.

Explain stage two like this:

"Now work in silence for a few minutes. Look at your notes and create some positive feedback for your partner. What is the upside of your partner's complaints? What are some potential positive outcomes that can be derived as a result of the situation your partner talked about?"

Allow two minutes for this step. When it looks like most are finished, give them three minutes to share with their partners what they wrote.

Discussion Questions

1. What surprised you about the results of this activity?

2. What did you think when you heard your complaints reframed?

3. What can you learn from this activity?

4. How can you use what you learned at work?

5. What was your biggest aha moment?

Mr. and Mrs. Wright

WHEN TO USE THIS GAME

As a fun way to start a meeting, to get everyone laughing, or to highlight the importance of active listening

OBJECTIVES

- To have fun and share some laughs with the team
- To illustrate the importance of active listening

Group Size

Any

Materials

One index card per person, pens or pencils

Time

10 minutes

Setting the Context

A 1984 study by researchers from the University of Texas at Austin found that in a typical conversation, most people remember only around 10 percent of what was actually said.[2] Fortunately, listening is a skill that can be improved with practice. Active listening is a useful communication technique where you consciously focus all your attention on the words and message of your partner. With practice, active listening can help us all become better communicators.

This quick energizer game challenges everyone to listen with focus and attention.

Preparation

None

---

2 Laura Stafford and John A. Daly, "Conversational Memory: The Effects of Recall Mode and Memory Expectancies on Remembrances of Natural Conversations." *Human Communication Research* 10 (Spring 1984): 379–402.

Procedure

Have everyone stand or sit in a circle. Give each person an index card and pen. Tell them to write their name on their index card. Tell the team: "I am going to read a story out loud to you. Whenever you hear 'right,' please pass your card to the person on your right. Whenever you hear 'left,' please pass the card to the person on your left. Listen carefully, because you will be passing the cards back and forth a lot! I promise I won't go too fast. Here we go.

This is a story about the WRIGHT family: Mr. and Mrs. WRIGHT, and their children Jimmy and Jennie WRIGHT.

One day the WRIGHT family decided to have a picnic at the park. 'There are only a few days LEFT of summer vacation,' said Mrs. WRIGHT, 'and it's a beautiful day to be outside!' The kids loved this idea because there was a big softball game at the park that day.

'What can we pack for lunch?' wondered Mr. WRIGHT. 'Well,' replied Mrs. WRIGHT, 'we have plenty of LEFTovers in the refrigerator. There's even some apple pie LEFT from the big bake sale!'

'Sounds good!' said Mr. WRIGHT. 'Apple pie is my favorite!'

They piled into the car and headed for the park. They had just LEFT when Jimmy cried, 'Uh-oh! I LEFT my softball glove back at home! Can we go back and get it?'

So Mr. WRIGHT got into the LEFT turn lane. He turned LEFT on Main Street and headed home. Unfortunately, the RIGHT lane was closed due to construction, so he took a quick LEFT on Elm Street, followed by one more LEFT on 5th Street. This took them RIGHT back home.

When they arrived, Jimmy hopped out of the car to get his glove. Just then Jennie remembered something. 'Be sure to bring my LEFT-handed glove, too!' she called to Jimmy. 'Last time, you only brought your RIGHT-handed one, and I was LEFT sitting on the bench all day!'

Jimmy went in the garage to get the gloves. He quickly grabbed his glove, but Jennie's LEFT-handed glove was nowhere to be seen! 'Where could it be?' he wondered. He ran to Jennie's bedroom to search for it, then the kitchen, then the backyard. And that's where Jimmy found Jennie's LEFT-handed glove, RIGHT in the backyard where she had LEFT it.

Jimmy hopped back in the car and they sped to the park with just moments LEFT to spare. The kids hustled out to the softball field. Jimmy WRIGHT took his place in LEFT field, and Jennie WRIGHT took her place at second base. Meanwhile, Mr. and Mrs. WRIGHT settled in to watch the game. Their picnic basket was full of LEFTovers, and they had quite a feast. It was an exciting game. The other team's LEFT-handed pitcher struggled against a string of RIGHT-handed batters and the score was tied all the way to the final inning. The game ended with Jimmy catching a fly ball to LEFT field, leaving Jimmy and Jennie's team undefeated for the season.

When they got home that evening, the kids had no energy LEFT and went RIGHT to bed. Mr. WRIGHT exclaimed to Mrs. WRIGHT, 'What a day! After all those LEFTovers, I need to go on a diet starting RIGHT away!' THE END.

Did you end up with your original card? Give yourself a round of applause if you did!"

Discussion Questions

1. What was most challenging about this activity?

2. What are some things that get in the way of good listening?

3. What can you do to become better listeners?

4. What are some things the team can do to improve everyone's listening?

5. On a scale of 1 to 10, with 10 being highest, how would you rate yourself as a listener? Why?

Our Team Standings

OBJECTIVES

- To get to know each other better and discover commonalities
  among team members
- To spark meaningful conversations about differences among
  team members

Group Size

Up to 20

Materials

A 50-foot length of rope or a roll of masking
tape

Time

20 minutes

Setting the Context

Strong, healthy work relationships lead to more effective teams. In your
work as a coach, make it your goal to help develop team members' abilities
to find common ground, appreciate differences, support one another, and
be candid about their own interests while being open to the concerns of
their peers.

Preparation

Mark a straight line approximately fifty feet long on the ground with the
rope or masking tape.

Procedure

Tell the team you will be asking them some questions that will reveal
things they have in common with each other, as well as uncover areas

where they differ. Some questions will be fun, some will be work related, and some will be a little more serious. The line on the ground represents your rating scale. Clarify for the team which end of the rope represents "low" and which end represents "high." For the questions where it's not necessarily a high or low, the notes in parentheses describe what each end represents. After each question you ask, have team members rate themselves by standing somewhere along the line.

Use your best judgment as team coach to ask questions that are meaningful for the group. Choose from this list, feeling free to change the wording or make up your own questions as you see fit.

- How do you feel about buttermilk? (Love it!...Gross!)
- How would you describe your work-life balance? (All work...All personal life)
- How do you feel about reality TV? (Love it...Hate it)
- How would you rate your capacity to contribute to your current project?
- How would you rate your understanding of the organization's vision?
- Line up based on who has the most unusual middle name.
- How would you rate your team's ability to manage conflict in a healthy way?
- How do you perceive the level of conflict on the team? (Nonexistent...High)
- How would you describe your feelings about change? (Love it...Hate it)
- How would you rate your understanding of where the team is headed?
- How often do you think about chocolate? (Never...All the time)
- Does your team have the resources it needs to accomplish your work?
- How clearly do you understand your role in the team?
- Line up according to how many years you have worked for the organization.
- How would you rate your understanding of your teammates' roles?
- Line up based on how passionate you are about sports.
- Line up according to who has traveled farthest from home.
- Line up based on how many books you have read in the past year.
- How spicy do you like your food? (Mild...Five-alarm fire!)
- Which mode of communication do you prefer most: face-to-face or 100 percent virtual?

This activity provides opportunities for some great discussion. For questions that are especially meaningful for the group, have team members gather into three small discussion groups based on where they ranked themselves. Those closest to one end of the spectrum will form the first group, those in the middle will form the second, and those at the opposite end will form the third. Have them discuss within their small groups why they ranked themselves the way they did and then have each group elect a spokesperson to share their group's response with the rest of the team.

Tips

- Keep things lively by including a mix of fun and serious questions throughout the activity.
- Finish on an upbeat note by asking a fun question.

Variations

Boost the energy level by allowing just ten seconds to line up for each question.

Push

When resistance or underlying conflict is felt

OBJECTIVES
- To increase awareness of our own reactions
- To choose an appropriate response in challenging situations

Group Size

Any, paired up with partners

Materials

None

Time

10 minutes

Setting the Context

The skill of *presence* is getting more challenging by the day. Cell phones, tablets, and laptops are with us everywhere we go, pulling our focus from what we are doing and breaking our concentration while we think. Coaching requires us to be in the moment. And choosing to be in the moment while coaching takes a commitment from every member of the team. Once we are present, we have the ability to observe our actions and reactions in real time. We create an opportunity to assess our reactions and choose appropriate responses. The bonus is that we open ourselves to more accurate interpretation of other team members' actions and reactions, enabling better communication to take place. Push is a simple, yet elegant activity that immediately reveals our natural responses to stress, conflict, competition, and change. You can use this activity in a variety of different situations to build awareness. Once aware, your team can begin to build their individual and collective EQ (emotional intelligence). With some additional training on EQ—awareness of self and self-management, awareness of others and relationship management—team members can help improve each other's individual EQ and the overall EQ of the team.

Procedure

Have team members form partnerships. Invite partners to stand and face each other, palms held chest-high and facing the other person. Ask partners to put their palms together. Say, "Look each other in the eye and decide which of the two of you has the darkest eyes." Allow a minute while they laugh and figure it out. Now say, "Dark-eyed person, these next instructions are for you only. Dark-eyed person, please gently and forcefully push against the palms of your partner." Allow a moment for everyone to do this. Now say, "Thank you, dark-eyed person, you may stop pushing." Repeat the same instructions, this time directed to the light-eyed person. After the light-eyed team members have finished pushing, say, "Thank you, everyone, now please drop your arms so we can observe what happened." At this point, stop for some mid-activity discussion questions.

Mid-Activity Discussion Questions

1. Does anyone remember what the instructions were?

2. Dark-eyed person, what did you do when you were asked to push?

3. Light-eyed person, what did you do when you were pushed?

4. Dark-eyed person, what did you do when you were asked to push?

5. Light-eyed person, what did you do when you were pushed?

6. When you were being pushed, what was your natural reaction?

7. How does this compare with your reactions to situations when you are challenged, in conflict, or in competition with another—either real or perceived?

8. Is there another way to respond?

9. Direct the team to go through this process once more, and this time, when the partners are being pushed, they should choose a different response. Direct the team through the process with the same instructions as the first time. You will notice a change in energy while the partners work together to choose and support other responses.

Final Discussion Questions

1. Was there a different response?
2. What did it look like?
3. What did it feel like?
4. When you feel pushed as you continue to work together, how else can you respond?
5. What does it take to get there?
6. Teams can be very effective at helping other team members increase their awareness; how would you like to be held accountable?

UFO Ball

WHEN TO USE THIS GAME

To begin creating a deeper level of connection to other team members and to the team itself

OBJECTIVES

- To differentiate a group from the team
- To solidify connections that make a team

Group Size

Any

Materials

One UFO Ball, which can be purchased at www.trainingwheels.com or by doing an online search for "UFO Ball" for other purchase options

Time

5 to 10 minutes

Setting the Context

Team has been defined as "a group of people who come together to achieve a common goal." It takes a group of people to make a team, but a team is much more than a group of people. A work team has a connection to the other members of the team and to the work to be done. The UFO Ball provides a great visual on the power of connections.

Preparation

None

Procedure

Invite the team to stand or sit in a circle. Tell them that the UFO Ball represents the work the team is responsible for doing. Present the UFO Ball to the person standing or sitting closest to you. Ask that person to take the ball from you and hold on to it with two fingers by placing one finger on the metal plate and the other finger anywhere else on the ball.

Then ask that person to make a connection with the person next to him or her by holding hands. Now ask the second person to connect with the person closest to him or her and on around the team until the last person (you) is connected to everyone else. Say, "At this point, we are all connected to each other. Let's see what happens when we all get connected with the work to be done." With your open hand, place one finger on the other metal bar on the ball and the other anywhere else on the ball. Do this in a way that your fingers are not touching the other ball-holder's fingers. The ball will immediately begin to flash and make noise. Allow time for the team to ooh and aah.

Begin asking the discussion questions. When you get to the third question, ask, "What happens when there is a break in our connection? Let's find out." Ask any two people in the team to break their connection. The ball will stop flashing until the connection is reestablished. Continue with the remainder of the discussion questions. Team members will have fun experimenting how connected they have to be for the ball to respond: can they simply touch fingers or do they have to hold hands?

Discussion Questions

1. What does it mean to be a team?

2. What is the value in being connected to the team?

3. How does it impact the team when there is a break in the collective connection?

4. What contributes to a feeling of connection?

5. What are some ways the team can become disconnected?

6. How can you help yourselves and others stay connected to each other and to your work?

What's in the Box?

To increase energy and creative thinking

OBJECTIVES
- To stimulate creativity and "out of the box" thinking
- To have fun and increase energy through action

Group Size

Up to 30

Materials

A medium- to large-size sealed cardboard box (big enough to be held with two hands but not so large as to be unwieldy), a sign inside the box that says "Your creativity," masking tape

Time

30 to 45 minutes

Setting the Context

This activity is a great way to energize the group at the beginning of a meeting or after a long break. It also stimulates creative thinking. This game uses the elements of improvisational theater and works great before a brainstorming session or as an afternoon energizer. It helps open the team up to a "possibilities conversation" and will generate some laughter and energy.

Preparation

Create the sign ahead of time and put it into the box and seal it. Place tape on the floor in two parallel lines about three feet apart and long enough to accommodate half of the participants standing on each line.

Procedure

Begin by saying, "Companies are often unable to create new ideas because of the confines they place themselves in. Thinking outside the box is required for reinvention. This game helps you envision solutions beyond what you would normally think of."

Divide the participants into two groups. Ask each group to stand on one of the lines, with both groups facing the same direction in a single-file line. Give the box to the participant at the front of one of the lines (Line A) and explain that the two groups will play a game called What's in the Box?

Explain the process as follows: "The participant at the front of Line B (without the box) will ask the participant holding the box (in Line A), 'What's in the box?' The participant holding the box (in Line A) will respond with a fictional answer as he or she hands the box to the participant asking the question in Line B."

The person now holding the box in Line B must react to whatever is "in the box." For example, a set of weights in the box would be extremely heavy. The participant who surrendered the box (Line A) now moves to the back of his or her team's line. The participant at the front of Line A repeats the question, "What's in the box?"

The participant at the front of Line B must respond with a different answer that relates to the first item supposedly in the box. For example, if a set of weights was the first item, smelly athletic shoes could be the next item, because you wear athletic shoes to lift weights. The participant at the front of Line B hands the box to the participant at the front of Line A and moves to the back of his or her line.

The participant in Line A, now holding the box, must react to the new item in the box. Repeat this process until everyone has taken one turn (if more than fifteen people) and two turns each (if fewer than fifteen). Ensure no one repeats an answer already given.

Invite everyone to be seated. Debrief the team on the experience, focusing first on their emotional reactions to the experience and then on the wide variety of items that were imagined to be in the box. Ask if they want to know what is really in the box. Open the box, displaying the sign that says, "Your Creativity."

Conclude by saying, "When we started this activity, your creativity was in the box. As you've seen, your creativity can't be contained by a box. You have been thinking outside the box, so your creativity is box-free! Let's keep the creativity going and unleash it toward our goal of [insert team goal here] and move into another game or a work-related project."

Rules

- Everyone must come up with an item inside the box that relates to the previous item mentioned.
- No item may be repeated.
- After handing off the box to the person asking, move to the end of your line.
- No one may open the box until the coach leads the debriefing session.

Discussion Questions

1. What did you enjoy about the activity?

2. How did it feel to come up with new items for the box?

3. What did you notice about how the items changed over time?

4. What conclusions can you draw from this?

5. What becomes possible when self-imposed barriers are removed?

Yes, But . . .

WHEN TO USE THIS GAME
To demonstrate the power of positive words and thoughts

OBJECTIVES
- To feel the impact of positive and negative words
- To get people thinking outside their comfort zone

Group Size
Up to 10
Materials
None
Time
15 minutes

Setting the Context
This game helps participants become more aware of how they inadvertently shut down others on the team. It provides a fun, safe way to demonstrate the impact their words have. It is a great game to use before brainstorming to highlight the point that all ideas are good ideas during brainstorming.

Preparation
Determine a topic, if you don't choose to use the one provided in the Procedure section.

Procedure
Ask for four to five volunteers. Tell this group (team one) that they are responsible for planning their company's annual awards celebration. Anyone on the team can start with the first suggestion for planning the event. Each of the subsequent ideas must start with, "Yes, but…" Continue the exercise until it runs out of steam.

Then ask for four to five more volunteers to form another group (team two). Tell them they are responsible for planning their company's annual awards celebration. Anyone on the team can start with the first suggestion for planning the event. Each of the subsequent ideas must start with, "Yes, and…." Continue the exercise for two or three minutes or until the group winds down.

Rules

- Team one must start all ideas except the initial idea with "Yes, but…"
- Team two must start all ideas except the initial idea with "Yes, and…"

Discussion Questions

1. How did it feel to have your ideas rejected? Accepted?

2. How did the energy in the room change during each exercise?

3. What causes a person to shoot down someone else's ideas?

4. How can you become more open to new ideas?

5

Creating a Vision

It's one of the characteristics of a leader that he not doubt for one moment the capacity of the people he's leading to realize whatever he's dreaming.

—Benjamin Zander

Bridges to Success

WHEN TO USE THIS GAME

Anytime, especially for teams starting a new project or engaging in some goal setting; also a great lead-in to a gap analysis session (see Setting the Context below)

OBJECTIVES

- To identify where the team is now and where it wants to be in the future
- To pinpoint the action steps necessary to take the team where it wants to be

Group Size

Any; split large groups into teams of 3 to 5

Materials

Scissors, disposable drinking straws, adhesive tape or masking tape, paper, sticky notes, pens or markers, a stapler, tape measure

Time

45 minutes

Setting the Context

This activity is a fun, lighter version of the useful organizational tool known as *gap analysis*. A gap analysis is a technique that helps teams identify the gaps between where they are now and where they want to be in the future. It also gives teams the opportunity to pinpoint the action steps that will help them get to where they want to be.

As a coach, use Bridges to Success as an interactive way to help the team identify its goals, gaps, and action steps, or as a lead-in to a full gap analysis session.

Preparation

Gather all the supplies before the group arrives. Provide each team with one pair of scissors, thirty drinking straws, a small roll of adhesive tape or masking tape, some paper, sticky notes, and pens or markers.

Procedure

Building the Bridges (30 minutes)

Split the group into work teams of three to five people each. Once the teams are created, pass out the building materials.

Tell the work teams they must each build a bridge that can support the weight of a stapler, using only the materials found in their building kits.

In explaining the rules to the teams, use this wording:

Rules

- Bridges must span the gap between two desks placed twenty inches apart. (If it's not possible to push desks together, use chairs, stacks of books, or reams of paper to create a twenty-inch gap.)
- Bridges may not be taped or secured to the desks in any way.
- Teams may only use the materials provided in the building kits.
- All teams must experience success.

Give teams a total of thirty minutes to build their bridges, divided into up to three rounds. Allow fifteen minutes for round one, ten minutes for round two, and five minutes for round three. (Note that some teams may not need all three rounds to successfully complete their bridges.)

At the end of each round, call time. Test each bridge to see if it can support the weight of a stapler placed in the middle. Add some fun and suspense as you slowly set the stapler down on the middle of each bridge. Encourage lots of applause from the rest of the group.

If necessary, move on to the next round, encouraging teams to revisit their designs and make whatever changes are necessary to strengthen their bridges. Teams may find it useful to consult or ask questions of the teams that were successful.

Call for a big round of applause after all teams have experienced success.

Connecting It to Real Life (15 minutes)

After the bridges have been built, tell the teams to take a few minutes of discussion time to identify a real-life goal that is important for the group. It's okay if each of the teams comes up with a different goal.

Next, using sticky notes or paper, have the teams label the parts of their bridges:

- Label one end of the bridge with the goal they have just identified. This represents "where we want to be."
- Label the other end of the bridge to represent "where we are now." This label should describe the current condition or state of the team. The difference between "where we are now" and "where we want to be" is the gap the team must cross to achieve success.
- Along the length of the bridge, label the tasks or action steps required to bridge the gap and achieve success. Be as specific as possible with this part, because detailed action steps are essential to success!

After they have finished labeling their bridges, invite each team to briefly share their results the rest of the group.

Tips

Place the bridges around your office or work site as a way to remind team members of their goal and the action steps they must take to get there.

Discussion Questions

1. In what ways was this process similar to your real-life project?
2. What changes did you make in order to build a strong bridge?
3. What did you learn from this activity?
4. Did anyone view this as a competition? Why or why not?
5. Did you ask for help from any of the other teams? Why or why not?
6. One of the requirements of this activity was that "all teams must experience success." What did you do to meet this requirement?
7. What are some ways you can help each other achieve success in real life?

"Coming Soon!" Movie Posters

WHEN TO USE THIS GAME

As an activity at the start of a project, when the team lacks clear focus about its goal, or when the roles of team members need to be defined

OBJECTIVES

- To create a powerful visual depiction of the team's goal
- To define the roles team members will play in achieving the goal
- To motivate team members by casting themselves as the stars, directors, and creators of their path to success

Group Size

Any; split large groups into teams of 4 to 5

Materials

One poster board and an assortment of colored markers for each team

Time

45 to 60 minutes

Setting the Context

An essential role of any coach is helping the team create a clear, focused goal. Equally important is for team members to understand the role each of them will play in achieving the goal. Without a clear-cut goal, a team may stumble along or become sidetracked. In the absence of well-defined roles, team members may end up duplicating one another's work, passing the buck, or not holding one another accountable.

This activity gives teams the opportunity to paint a clear picture of their goal and the individual roles each member will play, using Hollywood-style movie posters for inspiration.

Preparation

Most teams like to stand or sit around a table as they work on their posters, so allow plenty of work space for each team.

Procedure

Split the group into teams of four to five people each. Give each team a poster board and a set of colored markers. Tell them the object of the activity is for each team to create a Hollywood-style movie poster depicting their goal and casting all the team members in the story. Tell them that their posters should be as visually exciting as possible. Posters must include all the team members cast in the roles of "heroes," as well as depict their obstacles (for example, competitors, poor economic conditions, budget cuts) as "bad guys," and the team's "goal" (for example, $20 million in revenue within ten years) and other creative elements. For inspiration, teams can search online for images of current and classic movie posters.

Before they start creating their posters, encourage teams to spend some time discussing their actual "real life" goal and the roles everyone will play. Allow thirty to forty minutes for teams to plan and then create their posters. When everyone is finished, invite teams one at a time to share their posters with the rest of the group. Encourage teams to come up with creative ways to present their posters, perhaps by mimicking a theatrical movie preview or a Hollywood red carpet event. Give teams about five minutes to come up with their presentations, and allow about two minutes for each team to deliver their presentation.

Tips

Hang the teams' movie posters around the office or work site as a fun, constant reminder of their goal and the role every member plays.

Get It on the Table

WHEN TO USE THIS GAME

When you want to be sure everyone has an opportunity to engage in thoughtful dialogue on an important issue

OBJECTIVES
- To gain everyone's input and achieve consensus
- To discover attitudes, beliefs, and themes that are important to the group

Group Size

Any, paired up with partners

Materials

Small tables and chairs, butcher paper or flip-chart paper, colored markers or assorted sharpies, timing device, masking tape or painter's tape (optional)

Time

60 minutes

Setting the Context

This "team forum" brings out the team's commonalities and concerns as a way to achieve consensus and engage everyone in the conversation. The informal nature of the activity encourages everyone's input, generates fresh ideas, allows team members to build on one another's ideas, and helps them discover areas of agreement. For people who might be reluctant to share in the larger group, this encourages candid sharing of opinions, sparks a robust conversation, gets issues on the table in a less formal way, and generates a lot of thought.

Preparation

Choose the right question(s) to ask. This is the most important way to prepare for this activity. Take plenty of time to develop powerful question(s) that will drive lots of conversation. Powerful questions are simple and clear, open-ended, and thought provoking. They inspire people to dive deeper, discover possibilities, and invite inquiry and discovery.

Some good themes for creating your question could include: ways to resolve conflict, ways to appreciate differences, ways to lead, ways to encourage open sharing of knowledge, ways to build trust, ways to establish the team as collaborative, ways to improve the team's processes, ways to boost collaboration, ways to avoid "scope creep," ways to address new corporate initiatives or industry challenges, and so on.

Set the stage with care to create a positive, informal atmosphere that promotes deep, thought-provoking discussions. The conversation-based format for this activity is patterned after the World Café approach (theworldcafe.com). To set the stage, cover each table with butcher paper or flip-chart paper, place colored markers or sharpies on each table, and set each table with four chairs. Natural light and staggered tables provide a less formal feel. Consider placing flowers or candles on each table to simulate the café effect. Create a sign with the name of your café, for example, Idea Café, Communication Café, Leadership Café, Coach's Café, or Creativity Café. Display the topic question on either flip-chart paper or a PowerPoint slide so that everyone can see it.

Procedure

Invite the team members to sit down at one of the tables. There should be three or four people at each table. Explain the purpose for doing this activity, and present the question for discussion. Allow the group fifteen minutes to talk, discuss, explore, draw, and doodle all the aspects of the question. Tell them they are not necessarily looking for solutions, but opening new dimensions they may not have thought of before. At the ten-minute mark, ask the teams to identify three or more key ideas that have sprung from their discussion, and to get them "on the table" by either writing them down or drawing them. Challenge the tables to capture their ideas creatively. After all tables have captured their ideas, have each table choose a table host who will speak for the team.

Now instruct everyone to move to a new table, except for the table hosts, who will stay with their original table. Encourage team members to move randomly to new tables so that there is a fresh mix of people at each table. The table host will welcome the new members and offer a summary of what had been discussed before at the table, sharing the thoughts, words, and pictures of the previous group with the new participants. The conversation now continues, using the same question as before. This time, however, the new participants are encouraged to bring their ideas and blend them with what had been discussed before. The goal is to deepen the conversation, generate additional questions, and add new insights. Allow fifteen minutes for this round.

Repeat this process for one final round. Make sure that the same host remains at each table, and that everyone else moves to a new table with a fresh mix of people.

To end the activity, have each table host post his or her table's butcher paper to the wall and share the common ideas, themes, and questions that arose during the course of the three rounds. Follow with the discussion questions.

Discussion Questions

1. What common themes emerged?
2. How can you adapt what you learned for use in your "normal" team discussions?
3. How do ideas generated in this way differ from other ways of coming up with ideas?

Coach Note: For a more in-depth exploration of the World Café approach, visit the World Café website at theworldcafe.com.

In Order

WHEN TO USE THIS GAME

After you have developed trust within the team and the team is transitioning from forming to storming

OBJECTIVES

- To foster curiosity and questioning skills to build understanding
- To experience how different perspectives can come together

Group Size

Any; split large groups into teams of up to 12

Materials

One different picture for each team member

Time

20 to 30 minutes

Setting the Context

The storming stage of group formation is uncomfortable for most team members but is a necessary step to develop a trans-formed team. If you have laid the groundwork and established a healthy level of trust among team members, it's time to gently lead them into the skill of productive arguing. As team coach, this is a great responsibility, because team members will look to you for support and direction as they navigate this stage. This game opens the door to a lively discussion around healthy conflict and how team members would like to handle disagreements as they continue their work together. Fear of conflict can prevent a team from tapping into their creativity and becoming a truly transformed team, so time spent developing this skill is time well spent.

Using a game such as In Order facilitates a lively conversation, offering divergent perspectives. To solve In Order, the team must incorporate everyone's perspective to find the best solution, which leads a team to a collaborative outcome.

Preparation

You will need at least thirty to forty images for this exercise. Cut out a variety of photos from magazines and advertisements, or print images you find online. Choose images such as animals, nature, products, people, family life, buildings, and street scenes. Be sure to include images that may have several levels of meaning. For example, a family gathered around a meal could bring to mind "dinner" or "food" but could also bring to mind family, togetherness, or how to balance work and home life. Similarly, a photo of an expensive watch could suggest time or punctuality but could also represent luxury, success, or power.

Procedure

Shuffle the images and place them facedown on a table or the floor. Invite each team member to pick up one image or, alternatively, simply pass out one image to each person on the team. Ask participants to take a minute to look at their specific image and consider what message or story they derive from the picture. Allow one to two minutes of silence as they formulate their interpretations. Request that they hold that interpretation in mind as they move to the next step of the game. The next step is for the team to connect their images to build a story.

The challenge is for the team to line up in correct order based on the image they are holding. What is the story their images come together to convey? They will know if they are in correct order if they can tell a story that takes the listener easily from one image to the next. To do that, each person first needs to communicate his or her interpretation of the image he or she is holding. The team can then ask questions and discuss what ordering of the images makes the most sense. Can they change their interpretations? Yes! Encourage any and all creative ways in which to order themselves and their images to tell their story.

Variations

Give limited time for the team to connect their images to build a story. Limiting the time can lead to greater conflict—they are not only trying to make sense from seemingly disjointed ideas but are also working under pressure, which can lead to stress and conflict.

Discussion Questions

1. How did you organize your information?

2. Was a leader necessary?

3. How did your plan take shape?

4. Did your story change? If so, why? Is that okay?

5. What was the level of engagement of the team members? What are some reasons for this?

6. Did you experience any conflict? If so, how did you work through that?

7. How would you like to handle conflict on the team?

Mind the Gap

Anytime as a great exercise for teams starting a project or teams looking for ways they can be more effective; can be used repeatedly during the life of the team

OBJECTIVES
- To identify gaps between where the team is now and where they want to be in the future
- To establish action steps the team can take to get where they want to be

Group Size

4 or more

Materials

Masking tape or a length of string or rope

Time

30 minutes

MIND THE GAP

Setting the Context

Riders of the London Underground subway system are famously warned to "Mind the Gap." Signs and announcements implore train passengers to use caution as they step across the gap, or the space between the train door and the station platform. The gap is a danger zone...avoid the gap, or risk breaking a heel, twisting an ankle, or worse!

Every work team has its own set of gaps, meaning the differences between where the team is now and where it wants or needs to be in the future. Teams may experience gaps in technical skills like computer training or equipment maintenance; gaps in soft skills like leadership, communication, or customer service; or gaps in measurable things like sales figures, customer time on hold, or the time it takes to fulfill orders.

The team coach plays an important role in helping groups analyze and identify their gaps, and then mapping out the tasks and action steps necessary to bridge the gaps.

Preparation

Mark a straight line approximately fifteen feet long on the ground with masking tape or a length of string or rope.

Procedure

Have the entire team stand on one side of the line. Say to the team:

"Imagine we are standing at a train station, with the line on the ground representing the edge of the platform. The platform symbolizes where you as a team are right now. I will be calling out several categories. For each category I call out, please step off the platform by taking a step across the line toward an imaginary train waiting at the station. The train represents where the team needs to be. If you feel there is a big gap between where the team is now and where it needs to be, please represent that by taking a really big step from the platform to the train. If you believe there is little or no gap between where the team is now and where it needs to be, represent that by taking a very small step from the platform to the train."

Call out a category from the list below. Give everyone a few moments to reflect on the category, then have everyone take their step on the count of three.

After everyone has taken their step, invite team members to share the reason they took the step they did. Make note of categories where a majority of the team perceives wide gaps.

After you are done, review the categories with the team and have them identify the three that had the widest gaps. For each of these three categories, give the team a few minutes of brainstorming time to come up with a list of specific action steps or tasks they can do to close the gaps.

"Mind The Gap" Category List

Choose categories from the list that follows that make the most sense for your team. Feel free to change the wording or add your own categories if necessary.

Organization and Management

- Roles are clear.
- Job descriptions are in place.
- Team members have adequate training.
- We hold each other accountable.
- We treat each other with courtesy and respect.
- We trust one another.
- We manage conflict positively.
- We encourage one another.
- We seek feedback from one another.
- We encourage creative problem solving.
- Expectations are clearly stated.
- We celebrate our successes.
- Fun is a part of our work culture.

Equipment and Materials

- Equipment is properly maintained.
- Equipment is properly cleaned.
- Equipment instruction manuals are available.
- Procedures are in place for operation of equipment.
- Maintenance and cleaning records are kept.
- Maintenance and cleaning schedules are adhered to.
- Supplies are available.

Facilities and Premises

- Our workplace is clean.
- Our workplace is safe.
- Things are organized and easy to access.
- Common areas are kept clean and tidy.
- We keep the refrigerator clean and the candy dishes full.
- Lighting is ample for us to get our work done.
- The noise level is appropriate for the work we do.

Documentation

- We respond to emails in a timely manner.
- We assume positive intent when reading emails from other team members.
- We maintain adequate notes or minutes to drive actions forward.
- We are clear and concise in our communication.
- We communicate in the most appropriate way (email, face-to-face, phone, or conference call).
- We know where to access the documents or information we need.
- We keep our documentation up to date and organized.

Time

- We manage our time wisely.
- We set deadlines that are reasonable and appropriate.
- We stay focused on the goals we set.
- We start and end our meetings on time.

Money and Resources

- We have the resources we need to operate effectively.
- We work effectively within our budget.
- We manage our spending responsibly.

Staff Requirements

- We have enough staff to handle our workload.
- We have the right people in place.

Customer Service

- Staff has a solid knowledge of our business.
- Staff has a solid knowledge of our products and/or services.
- We project a professional image.
- We provide consistent service.
- Communication between staff and management is clear and open.
- Problems are anticipated.
- Team members build rapport with customers.

- Team members ask questions to understand customers' needs.
- Team members recommend the right solutions to customer problems.
- Team members respond to complaints effectively.
- Team members handle angry or unreasonable customers effectively.
- Staff deals with pressures and/or long lines positively.

Tips

Make the phrase "Mind the Gap" a part of the team's vocabulary. It's a fun way to build a mind-set of continuous improvement within the group.

Remind the group that gaps exist with every work team, and that gaps don't mean specific individuals are at fault.

Discussion Questions

1. Why did you take the size step you did?
2. What are the three biggest gaps for your team?
3. For the three biggest gaps, what are some action steps you can take to close each gap?
4. What gaps are you seeing that others are not seeing?
5. What gaps are others seeing that you are not seeing?
6. What do you as an individual need to do? What are you accountable for?
7. How can team members hold each other accountable?
8. What feedback can you provide each other to help stay on track?

Team Picture

WHEN TO USE THIS GAME

When starting a new team project

OBJECTIVES

- To design, define, and get buy-in to new project roles and responsibilities
- To think differently before diving into a new project

Group Size

Any

Materials

Flip-chart paper or poster board, masking tape or painter's tape, paper, colored markers, pens

Time

30 to 40 minutes

Setting the Context

Throughout the life of a team, there are often projects the team will undertake—projects with a deadline and specific goals. These projects give teams a wonderful opportunity to regroup and to design and define roles, expectations, and growth opportunities. They give a chance for team members to step out of their comfort zones and try something new in a supportive environment.

Preparation

Write the name of the project on the top of a flip-chart page or poster board and tape it to the wall.

Procedure

Explain the new project along with deliverables and time line. Ask team members to consider the new project and what role they would like to play on the project. Invite team members to step outside their current role and consider a role that may be a stretch or growth opportunity. Pass out the paper, markers, and pens. Ask team members to take two minutes to reflect on the question "What is your ideal role on this project?" to get clarity for their answer. Then ask them to draw a picture of that role along with any words that depict a clear picture of how they see themselves contributing to the project. Allow about ten minutes for this step of the process.

Once everyone is finished with their pictures, have them go up one at a time to tape their picture on the poster and present their desired role to the team. Six to eight pictures will fit neatly onto a poster board or flip chart, but it is okay if the pictures extend past the edges of the board. After all the pictures are on the poster, work with the team to organize the roles and responsibilities depicted in the drawings. Gather the team around the poster on the wall for this dynamic part of the process. If you have any roles that are the same, put the pictures on top of each other and group similar pictures together. Have team members step in to help rearrange the pictures. When this is done, you will have a clear picture of the roles and, more importantly, any gaps that are identified. Invite the team to look at the overall picture. Here are some questions to guide this part of the process: "What redundancies do you see? Are those redundancies needed for the success of the project? What roles are needed for this project that are missing from the poster? Are there any roles and responsibilities that are critical to this project that should be added to the drawings?" Based on the answers, have individuals add to or refine their pictures.

At this point, have team members create coaching partnerships. An example of a coaching partnership would be partnering with someone who is already proficient in the role another team member has chosen to take on. The learning partner would then ask the coaching partner questions that would help him or her to be successful. The coach's job is not to tell the learner what to do but rather to be open to answering the questions the learner asks.

After the partners work together, bring the team back together as a group for a discussion. This activity will be most effective if team members commit to supporting one another and checking in with each other on a regular basis.

Discussion Questions

1. Now that you have chosen your role and gained some insight, what else do you need to tackle this project?
2. What can support you?
3. What are you most excited about?
4. How can team members support each other going forward?
5. What are some ways you can check in with each other to make sure everyone is on track?

Name the Oracle

WHEN TO USE THIS GAME
To foster a collaborative environment

OBJECTIVES
- To increase collaboration
- To demonstrate the importance of listening

Group Size
Any
Materials
None
Time
15 to 20 minutes

Once

Upon

a

Time ...

Setting the Context
This is a fun and easy game to play that demonstrates the power of teamwork and collaboration and the importance of effective listening. No preparation or materials are needed.

Preparation
None

Procedure
Ask for four to six volunteers. Have them come to the front of the room and form a line, shoulder to shoulder. Tell them that they are "the Oracle" and have been imparted with the wisdom of the universe. They know all, see all, and will share all when asked. Tell the group members in the audience that this is their lucky day, because the Oracle can answer any question they have ever had. The key is that the Oracle may only speak one word at a time, by one team member at a time. Ask someone in the audience for a

question. Then start at one end of the Oracle and ask the first person to say one word to start a sentence to answer the question. The second person provides the second word, and so forth down the line, as each person adds one word until the thought is complete. If the sentence isn't finished, after the last person, the sentence goes back to the first person and back down the line as many times as needed. When the Oracle team feels the answer is complete, the last person will say, "Period," thus ending the sentence and the answer. Repeat until the Oracle has had a chance to answer several questions.

Rules
- Audience members may ask any question.
- The Oracle may only answer with one word spoken by one team member, in sequence, at a time.
- When the sentence is complete, the next Oracle member will say, "Period."

Discussion Questions
1. Ask the Oracle members, "How did that feel?"
2. Ask the audience, "What did you notice?"
3. What lesson can you learn from this?

Variations
If you have more than thirty people, you might want to break into groups of ten, with five people as the Oracle and five people in the audience, for more opportunities to participate and interact.

What Do We Want?

WHEN TO USE THIS GAME

To create a vision of the desired future

OBJECTIVES

- To move away from negativity
- To clarify what the future could hold

Group Size

Any

Materials

Colored construction paper, crayons, colored pencils or markers, flip-chart paper or large whiteboard and dry-erase markers, sticky notes

Time

30 to 60 minutes

Setting the Context

This game is a fun way to co-create the team's desired future.

Preparation

Have all of the materials available on a table. Think about a couple of key questions you want the team to answer or use the questions in the Procedure section.

Procedure

Say, "We are in charge of creating our team's future. I'd like each of you to take a piece of paper and a marker and draw a picture of how you see the team in three years. How are you operating? What are you doing? How does it feel to be part of the team? Or draw whatever comes to mind as you think about the team's future state. You will have ten minutes to draw. Artistic talent doesn't matter; stick figures are fine."

Once the drawings are complete, ask for volunteers to share their drawing and what it means to them. Post each on the wall after it has been discussed. Continue until everyone has shared.

Then, using the flip-chart paper or whiteboard, begin by asking, "What are the common threads?" Create three columns with the headings "What we want more of," "What we want less of," and "What we need to begin."

As each person shares an idea, encourage him or her to write it on a sticky note and post it in the appropriate column. Continue to ask for ideas until the team decides the column is complete.

Rules
- Because you are visioning, there is no judgment, there are no bad ideas, and nothing may be considered impossible at this point.
- Everyone contributes to the conversation.

Discussion Questions
1. What was it like to be part of this powerful conversation?
2. How have your feelings about the team's future state shifted since you started?
3. What will help you move to achieve this vision?
4. What would you like to tackle first?

Coach Note: A good option would be to use the Where's the Control? game (page 135) next. If so, keep the sticky notes created in this game to use in Where's the Control?

Yes!

WHEN TO USE THIS GAME

To demonstrate the power of positive words and thought

OBJECTIVE

- To feel the impact of full cooperation
- To get people thinking outside their comfort zone

Group Size

Any

Materials

None

Time

15 minutes

Setting the Context

This game helps team members become more open to suggestion and provides a fun, safe way to demonstrate the impact their words have. It is a fun game that lets people get loose and a bit silly, which helps the group bond. It is a great activity to use before brainstorming, to highlight the point that all ideas are good ideas during brainstorming.

Preparation

Create an open space in the room or outside. If indoor space is limited, be sure that any potential obstacles are removed to free up space.

Procedure

Ask everyone to stand, push in their chairs, and remove anything from the floor that might be tripped over. Or move the group outside. Tell them you will start by calling out a suggestion, for example, "Let's eat soup" or "Let's go swimming." They will enthusiastically shout "Yes!" and raise their hands to the sky and then begin pantomiming that activity as they move around the room. Tell them that after ten or fifteen seconds, anyone else can shout out another idea and the whole group will enthusiastically shout "Yes!" and raise their hands to the sky and then begin pantomiming that activity as they continue moving around the room. Continue this for several minutes. If people are hesitant, you may ask someone to select and shout out an idea.

Rules

- Whatever the suggestion, everyone is to shout "Yes!" and raise their hands to the sky.
- Continue moving around the space.
- All suggestions are valid.

Discussion Questions

1. How did it feel to have your idea accepted?

2. How did the energy in the room change during the exercise?

3. What did you learn about yourself?

4. How can you become more open to new ideas?

5. What can you take back to your "normal" team meetings?

6

Shaping the Plan

This time, like all times, is a very good one, if we but know what to do with it.

—Ralph Waldo Emerson

Marshmallow Challenge

WHEN TO USE THIS GAME

To explore creativity, free thinking, and teamwork

OBJECTIVES

- To build a tall, freestanding structure with specific supplies in a limited time
- To use teamwork and creativity to achieve the goal

Group Size

Any, split into teams of 5 or 6

Materials

A brown paper lunch bag for each team containing 20 sticks of uncooked spaghetti (not thin angel hair or thick fettuccine), one yard of string, one pair of scissors, and one regular-size marshmallow; one yard of masking tape per team; a slide or flip-chart page listing the rules; a timer or timing function on a big screen; a tape measure; optional: music, prizes

Time

20 to 30 minutes

Preparation

Place all of the materials inside the brown paper bag for each team, except the yard of masking tape; fasten the tape to the side of each team's table so it doesn't stick together. Post the rules.

Procedure

Explain the rules. State that the goal is to build the tallest freestanding structure out of the supplies provided. All supplies do not need to be used; however, the paper bag cannot be used and the marshmallow must be used in its entirety on top of the structure.

Review the posted rules at least twice. Some teams will want to cheat, so the clearer the rules, the better. Start the timer for eighteen minutes. Turn on the music, if desired. Provide time reminders at nine minutes, then at five minutes, three minutes, one minute, and thirty seconds and then a final energetic New Year's Eve–style ten-second countdown. Walk around the room observing patterns and activity. Provide encouragement and foster some friendly competition. Remind them that the structure must be freestanding. When time is called, ask everyone to be seated so that all the structures can be seen. Start to measure the standing structures from shortest to tallest. If keeping score, ask someone to capture the heights on a flip chart or notepad. If a prize is offered, it goes to the team that has built the tallest freestanding structure. The prize could be a standing ovation.

Rules

- Use as much or as little of the kit contents, though the paper bag may not be used.
- The spaghetti, string, and tape can be broken or cut as desired.
- The entire marshmallow must be on top of the structure. If the marshmallow is cut or eaten, the team is disqualified.
- The structure must be freestanding; it cannot be suspended from a light fixture or other object. This is cause for disqualification.
- At the end, the structure must be freestanding, in that no team member may hold on to it for stability. This is cause for disqualification.
- The challenge will run for eighteen minutes.

Discussion Questions

1. What assumptions did you make?
2. What supported your success?
3. What got in the way?
4. How did you work as a team?
5. It has been shown that kindergarten students create better, taller structures than business school students. Why do you think that is true?
6. What lessons can you learn from this game that are transferable to our working environment?

Coach Note: For more information, review the entire activity and background information at www.MarshmallowChallenge.com.

Pass the Buck

To have people learn more about cooperation and handling competing priorities

OBJECTIVES

- To get people working together
- To have fun and increase energy through action

Group Size

Up to 12 people

Materials

Stopwatch or timer; a one-dollar bill; a variety of objects of different sizes, textures, and weights, such as coins, bag of candy, full water bottle, stapler, magazine, tennis ball, thumb drive, open coffee mug filled halfway with water, baseball cap, keys, sunglasses

Time

15 minutes

Setting the Context

This is a fun, energizing game to get people working together. Play this game anytime you want to recharge energy levels. This game is particularly applicable to work because the team must increase the pace, set higher productivity standards, and look for opportunities to improve the process.

Preparation

Gather the supplies ahead of time. Make sure you have enough objects so that everybody gets one.

Procedure

Invite the team to form a circle either seated or standing. Pass out the objects so everybody gets one, making sure someone has the dollar bill. This person will be known as the "buck holder."

Tell the team: "The goal of this activity is to pass your set of objects around the circle three times. Everybody must start the game with one item. The person with the dollar bill, or the 'buck holder,' will be the starting and stopping point for scoring. I will be your official timekeeper. When I say 'Go,' start passing the items around the circle. After the buck has made three complete circuits, call out 'Done' and I will stop the timer. If any item drops, you must start the process again."

Play one round to establish a benchmark. Then challenge the group to decrease their time by 20 percent. For example, if their time was 100 seconds, their new challenge will be to shave 20 seconds off their score, making their new time goal 80 seconds. Give the team two minutes before the round begins to brainstorm ways to improve their score. Play the second round and announce their time.

Play a third and fourth round, challenging the team to set even higher standards. Ask, "Can you continue to improve?" Allow some time for the team to set their own standard for these rounds and to brainstorm some new ideas.

Rules

- Everyone must touch and pass every object.
- The person with the one-dollar bill (the "buck holder") is the starting and stopping point for measuring the time.
- If an object is dropped, you must start over.

Discussion Questions

1. How did it feel handling the various objects? Were some easier than others?

2. What did you learn?

3. How is this like "raising the bar" at work or in your industry?

4. How is this similar to the way you approach challenges at work?

5. What innovations occurred?

Coach Note: Pass the Buck is transferable back to the team's work by focusing on the behaviors and skills that are practiced in the game. If one object can hold some of the other objects, a team may want to attach or combine them. You will determine if this is acceptable or not. If it comes up, include it in the debriefing.

Picture This!

WHEN TO USE THIS GAME

At the start of a new project or to help break a project down into specific action steps

OBJECTIVES

- To create a visual depiction of the team's project or goal
- To identify the action steps they must complete to achieve the goal

Group Size

Up to 20

Materials

Plenty of paper, pens and markers

Time

30 to 45 minutes

Setting the Context

This activity is inspired by *Zoom,* a lovely children's book by Istvan Banyai. *Zoom* contains no words, only a series of colorful illustrations that create the effect of a camera slowly zooming out to provide a new perspective. Each illustration reveals important new details and connects to the next page in a logical, cohesive way. If just one illustration is left out, the story falls apart. It's a wonderful metaphor for work projects that require multiple, sequential steps to complete.

Preparation

None

Procedure

Have team members think about a current goal or project to which they are collectively committed. Tell them to envision what it will look like when the goal has been reached or the project completed. Next, have them consider all of the action steps they must take to get from where they are now to their desired end state. For this activity, they will be creating a picture book that visually depicts their action steps in a series of drawings or doodles that lay out their plan from start to finish. Have the team follow these instructions in creating their picture book:

1. Create a drawing or doodle depicting where you are right now. If words are necessary, use them sparingly. This will be the first page of your book.
2. Create a drawing or doodle depicting your goal achieved or your project completed. Again, use words sparingly. This will be the last page of your book.
3. Now draw a set of pictures showing all the intermediate steps that will get you from page one to the final page of your book. Use all the paper you need, making sure that each page depicts one specific action step. Words should be used sparingly, if at all.

Split up the workload, assigning two to three people to illustrate each page.

If certain action steps are to be performed by specific individuals, be sure to label or depict them in your pages. Each drawing or doodle should be detailed enough so that anyone on the team can easily understand the action step shown on each page.

Encourage the team to spend some time planning and discussing their goal and action steps before they start illustrating their book. Make sure every member of the team contributes to the drawings, reminding everyone that no one will be judged for artistic ability!

After they have finished, have the team review their book and summarize the action steps they have created. Finally, put all the pages in the correct order and hang them around the office or share them via email as described on the next page.

Tips

Bring a copy of *Zoom* to your meeting, and share it with the team prior to starting this activity.

Have the team do the Zoom activity found in *The Big Book of Low-Cost Training Games* by Mary Scannell and Jim Cain.

Post the team's action step drawings around the office, and have them celebrate after each step has been completed.

Scan all the pages and email a copy of the book they have created to everyone in PDF format.

Discussion Questions

1. How was this exercise helpful to your team?
2. Did you end up with more or fewer action steps than you originally anticipated? Why or why not?
3. What action steps or potential problems did this activity uncover that you had not originally considered?
4. Does everyone on the team fully understand the steps necessary to achieve the goal or complete the project?
5. What are some ways you can keep one another accountable for your areas of responsibility?

Speed Sort

WHEN TO USE THIS GAME

To discover team members' natural response to working under pressure

Group Size

6 to 15, split into teams of 3 to 4

Materials

Three decks of playing cards per team

Time

25 to 30 minutes

Setting the Context

Working under pressure reveals a lot about a team. Do team members react to pressure and stress or do they become aware of themselves and others to choose an effective response? Do they communicate effectively or shut down?

Preparation

None

Procedure

Have the group split into competing teams of three to four people each. Give each team three decks of playing cards and instruct them to completely shuffle all the decks together to create a single big stack of cards. Tell them that they will be competing to see which team can sort their cards fastest with no mistakes. The goal is to put the cards back together into three complete, separate decks of cards. Each deck must contain all four suits (hearts, clubs, diamonds, and spades), and each suit must contain all the cards of that suit arranged in ascending order (ace, 2, 3, 4, 5, 6, 7, 8, 9, 10, jack, queen, king).

Give the teams a few minutes to plan and strategize before starting.

Restate to the teams that they must sort their cards with no mistakes, then say "Go!" and let the race begin!

In your role as team coach, pay attention to how people interact within each of the teams. For example, some teams may brainstorm to come up with an effective game plan, while other teams may be overly eager to begin and skip the planning phase completely. See if you notice any connections between what happens in the planning phase and how well teams perform during the actual race.

After the teams finish the race, inspect the fastest team's cards to see if they were sorted correctly. If they were, declare them the winner! If they were not, move on to the next fastest team and inspect their cards. Continue doing this until you find the winning team.

Discussion Questions

1. How did you do as a team?
2. Did you come up with a strategy during the planning phase? What was it?
3. How well did the team execute your strategy?
4. Describe any setbacks or challenges your team experienced. How did you respond?
5. Did the fact that this was a race affect your team's performance? In what ways?
6. Were any roles assigned, or did any roles emerge during the activity?
7. What effect does working under pressure have on your team in real life?
8. What lessons can you learn from this activity that are meaningful for your team?

Coach Note: Use decks of cards that are similar in size and color to increase the challenge level. Use decks of different size and color to decrease the challenge level. With multiple teams, be consistent with their decks.

Tallest Tower

WHEN TO USE THIS GAME
To reignite a team's commitment to working together

OBJECTIVES
- To consider the things that enhance and hinder teamwork
- To build effective communication and collaboration skills

Group Size

A minimum of 6; two teams of at least 3 people

Materials Required

Building blocks/bricks that can be hooked together such as the Lego brand and one base for each team of 3 to 6 people, tape measure, timer, pen and paper

Time

30 to 40 minutes

Setting the Context
Collaboration and teamwork are essential components of effective teams. When team members find themselves overwhelmed by a task or a deadline, it is not uncommon for them to put their heads down and get to work, forgetting they have a team to support them. This activity is the springboard to an in-depth discussion on a team commitment to working together.

Preparation
Divide the blocks into equal parts so that each team has the same number of and same shape blocks to work with. About 150 Lego bricks for each team is a good number.

Procedure

This three-part activity focuses on collaboration, teamwork, and the importance of communication. The level of partnership and teamwork is increased incrementally with each part of the exercise, which allows team members to compare results as they work more collaboratively.

Begin by asking the team, "What does is look like when people work effectively together? What does it feel like when people work effectively together?" Spend about five minutes discussing the look and feel of an effective team.

Next, split the group into at least two different working teams. The ideal number for a working team is three to six people. Give each team one set of bricks and one building base. You can easily find these materials online (or borrow them from your children).

Introduce the activity. Each team will use the materials to build the tallest tower they can with the materials provided. Let each team know they have the same amount of bricks to complete the project. Explain that this activity has three rounds, and that each round has a different level of teamwork.

Round One

Say: "Each group must build the tallest tower possible using only the bricks provided to them. In this round, you are not allowed to communicate with each other verbally or in writing. You have ten minutes to build your tower."

After ten minutes, measure and record the height of each team's tower. Lead a five-minute discussion asking these questions:

- How satisfied are you with your results?
- How did the lack of communication impact your ability to work together effectively?
- Describe how you set about accomplishing your task.
- Did you work individually or as a team?
- Did you cooperate or compete? Why?
- Could you have done better? What would you change?

Ask groups to dismantle their towers to get ready for the next round.

Round Two

Say: "In this round, you may communicate in any way you choose. Your team needs to build another tower; the goal is to build this second tower taller than your first one. You will have ten minutes to build your new, taller tower."

In this round, teams usually finish before the time is up. When all teams are finished, again measure and record the height of each team's tower. Compare these results to those from round one. Lead another five-minute discussion asking these questions:

- How satisfied are you with your results this time?
- What was different about how you accomplished your task in round two?
- What did you notice about the level of cooperation and energy during this round?
- What does it sound like or what do you hear when people work together effectively?
- How does this compare to teams who are not working together effectively?
- From this, what could your team do to be more effective together?

Ask groups to dismantle their towers to get ready for the next round.

Round Three

Say: "In this final round, you are all one big team and may combine your resources. That is, you can use all the bricks from all the teams and as well as the collective knowledge and experience you gained in rounds one and two. You only have ten minutes for this final round, so please keep track because you need to self-manage your time."

After ten minutes, make a big show out of measuring the new collaborative tower and comparing the results to those from the previous rounds. Lead the final debriefing discussion with these questions:

- How did you organize your larger workforce?
- How did you manage to take advantage of the extended workforce?
- Did you borrow ideas from groups who performed better in previous parts or did you put certain individuals in charge based on their past performance?

- Do you think you were more successful as a larger team, or do you think it was more efficient to work in smaller teams such as in round two?
- You identified specific things about the way an effective team looks, feels, and sounds; how did you see those things demonstrated during this round?
- What did you learn about working together effectively?

Where's the Control?

WHEN TO USE THIS GAME
To understand what is within the team's control

OBJECTIVES
- To move away from negativity
- To focus on what can be achieved

Group Size
  Any
Materials
  Flip-chart paper, markers, one set of Where's the Control? Cards, scissors, tape
Time
  15 minutes

Setting the Context
This is an excellent way to focus the team on what is within their sphere of control and influence.

Preparation
Have all materials available. Draw the grid below on a flip-chart page. Reproduce and cut up one set of Where's the Control? Cards.

Procedure
Unveil the flip-chart page as you begin the activity. Say, "We as human beings often spend a significant amount of time talking about what's wrong and how we are helpless to improve or change things. Yet there is often quite a bit that is within our control or influence. Let's look at some items and determine which is which."

Explain that you will read one of the cards and the group will discuss whether it is within the team's control (one or all of the team members can impact this), within the team's influence (they can talk with someone or influence another to take action), or outside their control.

Read the first card and engage the group in discussion. (**Hint:** Sometimes the discussion is far more valuable than the actual card placement as it shows where there is optimism, pessimism, strength, etc.) When there is disagreement, continue the discussion until the group agrees where the card should go.

Rules:
- Every item goes onto the flip chart.
- Everyone contributes to the conversation.

Discussion Questions
1. What was it like to be part of this conversation?

2. What did you notice about how you view things?

3. How might this help you on future projects?

Coach Note: If you choose to use this game after What Do We Want? (page 115), use the sticky notes from that activity rather than the cards provided in this game.

Where's the Control?

Within our control	Within our influence	Out of our control

Where's the Control? Cards

A hurricane
Healthy eating
Length of team meetings
Next year's team budget
Saving money
Federal legislation affecting our industry
Improving literacy of children in our community
Visibility of our team within our organization
Having fun at team meetings
Company sales
Improving the skills needed for our jobs
Customer service
Eating ice cream on Tuesday
What time my workday ends
What I wear to work
When I eat lunch

7

Executing the Game Plan

Purpose always serves—it is the manner in which we use our gifts to make a difference in the world. Purpose is not purpose without adding value to others. It is not self-expression for its own sake; it is self-expression that creates value for those around you.

—Kevin Cashman

All for One

When team members put their own success before the team's success

OBJECTIVES

- To reset the team as a team
- To open a discussion on team loyalty

Group Size

Any

Materials

One 16-foot length of rope; a variety of different size and type balls, for example, tennis balls, small rubber bouncy balls, inflated beach balls, marbles (one ball per person); bucket

Time

10 to 20 minutes

Setting the Context

As the team goes about getting their work done, there will be times that team members will consciously or unconsciously put themselves and their individual accomplishments ahead of those of the team. This game can be used in the forming stage, but it may be much more effective in the performing stage to reset the team as a team and remind individuals that they are a part of something bigger. At the very least it allows team members to openly discuss the fundamentals of a team; it's a great "back to basics" activity.

Preparation

Tie the ends of the rope together to form a rope circle and place it on the ground. Place the balls in a bucket for easy transport. For best results, you will need a large space for this game.

Procedure

Invite team members to spread out on the outside of the rope circle. Once the team is in position, ask them to reach down and pick up the rope using both hands. At this point you are looking for the team to form a large circle with the rope, where they are evenly spaced around the circle. Walk around the circle with the bucket of balls, requesting that each team member remove one hand off the rope to take one ball. Each team member should now have one ball in one hand and be holding the rope with the other hand.

Once everyone has a ball, tell the team to put the rope back on the ground, take five large steps away from the outside of the rope, put their ball on the ground, and come back to their original position and pick up the rope again.

Now they are in position to begin the game.

To simulate what can happen to the team dynamic when individual team members are feeling pressure from short deadlines and time constraints, use the following wording when introducing this game.

Say: "On my 'go,' everyone needs to retrieve their ball without letting go of the rope. One, two, three, go!" Say this quickly without giving the team any time to plan or to even consider options.

Now, as team coach, pay close attention to the team dynamics. Will they scramble to get their ball, dragging the rest of the team along? Will they let go of the rope and run to get their ball? Will they work together to self-organize to form an easy plan to retrieve all the balls one by one, ensuring a "win" for the team as a whole? Whatever they do is an excellent barometer for their loyalty to the team and can make for an excellent discussion that will either validate their chosen process (if they worked together) or allow the team to become aware of the challenges of keeping loyalty to the team when we are feeling pressure to perform individually.

Discussion Questions

1. How did the sense of urgency contribute to the way you went about the activity?

2. In what ways does this reflect the way you get our work done under time pressures or tight deadlines?

3. If you had to do it again, what would you do differently?

4. What can you learn about yourselves from a game like this?

5. How can you improve your team based on the experience you created during the game?

6. What can you do to become a more effective team member?

7. How would you like to be held accountable to that commitment?

Broken Squares

WHEN TO USE THIS GAME

To help the team develop a spirit of cooperation, or if team members are holding back ideas or resources, or keeping their guards up to the point that it is detrimental to the team

OBJECTIVES

- To work together to achieve a common goal
- To explore the behaviors that affect the team's success

Group Size

6 to 16

Materials

Broken Squares Puzzles cut out of cardstock or poster board (patterns provided), markers, scissors, five large envelopes, six copies of the Broken Squares Team Instructions handout

Time

30 to 35 minutes

Setting the Context

For the good of the team and the organization, it's beneficial for team members to expand their scope, realizing their work is part of a bigger picture.

Preparation

Create the five Broken Squares Puzzles out of heavy cardstock or poster board (see the template that follows). Each square should be approximately six inches. After you have cut up the puzzles into pieces, mix the pieces of all five puzzles together, and place five randomly selected pieces into each of the five envelopes.

Procedure

The group should elect one person to play the role of observer. This person will not be on a team and will not participate in the game. The observer's role is described in the Broken Squares Team Instructions handout that follows. Then have the group split into five work teams of one to three people each. Balance the work teams as evenly as possible so they have about the same number of people. Make sure to allow a few feet of space between each of the work teams.

Read aloud to the group all the information contained in the Broken Squares Team Instructions handout, then give the observer and each work team a copy of the handout to refer to during the activity.

After all the work teams get a copy of the handout, pass out the five envelopes. Say to the group: "You have twenty minutes to achieve the goal. You may begin now."

At the end of twenty minutes, call time. Collect all the pieces and debrief the experience using some of the discussion questions below. Be sure to ask the person who played the role of observer to share his or her observations about how the team performed together.

Discussion Questions

1. How did this activity challenge you?
2. How would you describe the group's level of cooperation?
3. How willing were you to give away pieces? Why?
4. Did everyone stay fully involved throughout the process? Why or why not?
5. Did you notice anyone dominating the activity? If so, what effect did it have on the team?
6. Did anyone notice frustration or impatience during the process? If so, what effect did it have on the team?
7. Were there any aha moments or important turning points for the group?
8. What can this activity teach you about working together in real life?

Broken Squares Team Instructions

Your group has been split into five work teams. Each work team will receive an envelope containing several puzzle pieces. Once the facilitator tells you to start, you may begin working to achieve the goal described below.

One person from the group will play the role of observer. This person will not participate in the activity. The observer's job is to simply watch what happens and make sure everyone follows the rules. If someone breaks a rule, the observer may intervene to warn that individual.

The Goal
The goal will be achieved when there is a perfect square, each of the same size, in front of each work team.

Rules
- No one is allowed to talk or communicate in any way. The use of gestures, facial expressions, or body language to communicate is forbidden.
- No one may ask for a piece from another person, or use gestures or body language to indicate that he or she wants a piece.
- However, anyone may give a piece to anyone else, from any team, at any time.
- You may not place your pieces in the middle area for other people to take.
- You may use only the puzzle pieces provided.

Broken Squares Puzzle Template

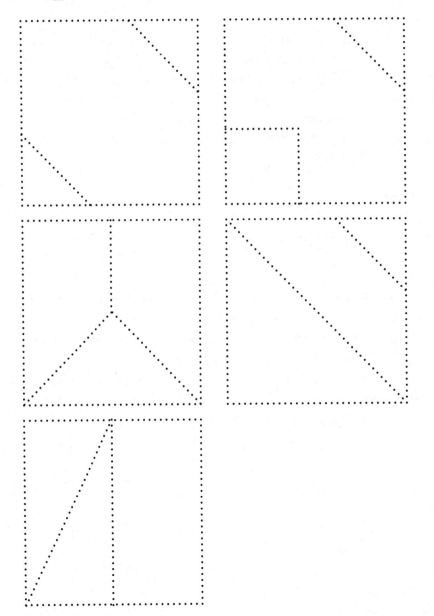

Go

WHEN TO USE THIS GAME

When team members are blaming others on the team for the team's failures

OBJECTIVES

- To consider another perspective
- To build and practice questioning skills

Group Size

Any

Materials

None (Optional: masking tape or place markers)

Time

20 to 30 minutes

Setting the Context

Even the best teams don't like to fail. Even the best team members sometimes blame others for the mistakes of the team. We all like to think we are willing to be held accountable, but if we are relying on someone else to do our job effectively, we sometimes fall short. This is a dynamic game that demonstrates that the team fails together and succeeds together and that everyone has something to contribute for the team to be successful.

Preparation

An open area is required with enough space so the team can stand in a circle with about an arm's length between each person. Make sure team members are equally spaced. While no materials are necessary, you may choose to use masking tape or place markers to create the circle beforehand, placing a marker where you would like each person to stand.

Procedure

Once the team is standing in a circle, explain to them that when the game begins, the only word anyone is allowed to speak is the word "Go." The word "Go" can only be said after making eye contact with someone across the circle. You will begin by standing in between two of the equally spaced team members, but you will not have an official spot in the circle. Tell the team that to get the game started, you will make eye contact with someone from across the circle to get his or her attention with the intent of getting that person to say "Go" so that you may leave your space and start the game. When one person says "Go" to you, which can only be said after making eye contact, you will start walking at a slow pace toward the person who told you to go. The challenge is for the person who told you to go to make eye contact and get someone to tell him or her to go *before* you get to his or her spot. At this point, before playing, go over the rules.

Rules

- Nothing can be said besides the word "Go."
- Only one person can occupy a spot at a time.
- You may not leave your spot unless someone has told you to go, and only after you've told someone else to go.
- You may only say "Go" if you have made eye contact with the person who needs your help so that he or she can move out of his or her spot.
- If a person tries to occupy a spot before the spot holder has time to get someone else to tell him or her to go, the round ends.
- After reading the team the rules, say, "Let's get started" and start the game by getting someone to make eye contact with you and say the word "Go."
- If a person attempts to enter a spot before the spot holder has time to get someone to tell the spot holder to go, the round ends. Take that opportunity to allow the team to assess their strategy and make any adjustments or plans. Continue with additional rounds until the team understands the process and can get the team moving in a fluid motion and everyone has had a chance to "Go."

Discussion Questions

1. What was challenging or frustrating about this game?

2. When mistakes were made in early rounds, who was to blame?

3. How important was it to have a plan?

4. Once you had a plan, were you immediately successful? Why or why not?

5. What did "help" look like in this game?

6. What did it take for the team to succeed?

7. How does a game like this relate to working better together?

Lemons to Lemonade

WHEN TO USE THIS GAME

After team members have gotten to know each other and some trust has been established

OBJECTIVES

- To increase trust and create a supportive team climate
- To become comfortable asking for help and feedback from one another

Group Size

Any; split large groups into teams of 4 to 5

Materials

Slips of paper and pens

Time

30 to 45 minutes

Setting the Context

It can be a big risk to ask for help at work. Many people fear that seeking help in the workplace will make them look stupid or cause them to be seen as weak or indecisive. As a result, costly mistakes may be made and great ideas may never see the light of day. A healthy level of trust among team members can result in much more positive outcomes. Teams with a trusting and supportive climate allow members to seek out ideas and input from each other without fear of judgment. Great ideas, fewer costly mistakes, and better ways of working together happen on teams where people are not afraid to ask for help.

Preparation

If you will be splitting the group into smaller teams, be sure to provide enough space between the teams for them to have their own semiprivate discussion areas.

Procedure

Split a larger group into teams of four to five people each. Ask team members to think about a work-related situation they wish they had handled differently at some point in their career. Tell everyone to anonymously write on a slip of paper a description of the circumstances surrounding the situation, but to avoid describing their actual response. Have someone from each team collect the slips of paper, then draw one randomly and read it aloud to the rest of the team. Allow each person from the team to then share suggestions or good ideas that could have led to a better outcome. After everyone has contributed their suggestions and ideas, have the team decide which response would lead to the best result.

Repeat this process for each of the situations described by the team members, making sure to allow time for everyone to share their good ideas and best practices.

Variations

For teams with a high level of trust, have team members simply share their situations aloud to their team instead of writing them on slips of paper.

Discussion Questions

1. How does this activity benefit the team?
2. What keeps people from asking for help or advice?
3. What can team members do to make it easy to ask for help from one another?
4. Does anyone have a current situation where he or she could use some help or advice from teammates? Allow time for anyone who wishes to share his or her situation and for teammates to offer their ideas and suggestions.

Red or Black

To have people learn more about cooperation and competition

OBJECTIVES
- To get people working together
- To look at cooperation and competition

Group Size

6 or more

Materials

A deck of playing cards, flip chart and markers,
timer

Time

30 to 40 minutes

Setting the Context

This is a quick, visual way to demonstrate
the importance of cooperation versus competition. It is also helpful to look
at the assumptions the teams make.

Preparation

Create a flip-chart page for the scoring. Have one heart and one club card
for each team. Divide the group into teams of three to five. Ideally, you
want at least three players per team to allow for robust dialogue as the
teams decide which color to choose.

Red/Black Scoring Chart

Round	Team A	Team B	Team C
1			
2			
3			
4			
5			
Total			

Procedure

Split the group into three (or more) teams of three to five people. Have the teams move to different areas of the room. Explain that the teams will play five rounds of Red or Black. In each round, each team must decide to choose a red or a black card. Give each team one red card (hearts) and one black card (clubs).

You will give the teams two minutes to discuss their choices. Give them a thirty-second warning (you can extend the time later in the game if there are robust discussions). Then say, "Choose one person to hold up the card displaying the color your team chose. When I count to three, each group will have one person hold up the team's chosen color. One, two, three."

To score the teams, look at the cards each team chose. If every team chooses black, each team scores 50 points. If only one team chooses red, that team scores 100 points and the others score 0. If more than one team chooses red, all teams score 0.

The goal is to score as many points as possible (do not mention anything about competition among the teams, only that the goal is to score "as many points as possible"). Record the scores after each round. After all five rounds have been played, total the scores for each team.

Discussion Questions

1. Were you competing with each other?

2. Did you discuss the instructions within your team?

3. What factors impacted your choices?

4. When did you realize it was in the best interest of the team to cooperate?

5. How can you anchor this learning back to your work environment?

Coach Notes: This is a great complement to the All for One game (page 141); they are thematically similar. Yet often the lessons learned from one game may not be remembered as you move into the next game. If using both, during the second debriefing, ask, "What was originally learned? How did you use or forget that learning as you played the second game?" Another variation would be to have one person be the leader for each team and that person would choose the color without group discussion. (If using this option, make it a rule.) Then debrief by asking, "What impact did letting a team leader choose the color have?"

Sticking to the Goal

WHEN TO USE THIS GAME
Before the team sets new goals

OBJECTIVES
- To work in sync toward a common goal
- To exercise leadership and communications skills

Group Size
Any; split large groups into teams of 5 to 10

Materials
A roll of strong, high-quality duct tape, a sheet of paper per team, pens or markers

Time
15 to 20 minutes

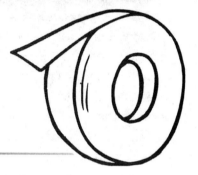

Setting the Context

Teamwork is the ability to work together toward a common vision. The ability to direct individual accomplishment toward organizational objectives. It is the fuel that allows common people to attain uncommon results.

—Andrew Carnegie

Sticking to the Goal is a fun activity that requires team members to work together to achieve a shared goal. It also provides coaches a great opportunity to observe how the team organizes itself, which team members step into leadership and support roles, how well the team communicates, and how team members deal with setbacks.

Preparation

Create a starting line and a finish line on the floor using duct tape. The distance between them should be about twenty-five feet. Make each line about ten feet long. Divide larger groups into teams of five to ten people.

Procedure

Give each team of five or ten people a few minutes to discuss and agree on a real-life work goal that is shared by everyone on that team. Have them write that goal on a piece of paper, then tape it to the floor or wall just past the finish line.

Have everyone stand behind the starting line. Tell the group:

"Now that you've agreed on a common goal, your challenge is to work in sync to successfully reach it. For this activity, your whole team must move together as a group until everyone crosses the finish line representing your goal. Unfortunately, no one's feet may physically touch the ground between the lines. To make it across successfully, you will need something to stand on! Unroll two long strips of duct tape about eight to ten feet long and place them on the ground sticky side up, parallel to each other just like a pair of skis. Form a single-file line and have everyone on your team place his or her left foot on the left ski and right foot on the right ski. Make sure that each person's entire foot, heel to toe, stays stuck to the duct tape all the way to the finish line. You will need to communicate effectively and step in sync to make it to your goal. Good luck!"

After you have read this to the team, give them a few minutes to plan and strategize before starting. Once they are ready to begin, restate the rules, along with a few safety reminders:

Rules

- Teams must not rip the duct tape. If a ski rips, the team must go back to the starting line and tear off a new piece of duct tape to replace it.
- Everyone's entire feet (heel to toe) must stay stuck to the duct tape until the team crosses the finish line.
- Everyone must wear shoes to participate in this activity. Sandals are not allowed.

- Each team should designate at least one person to take the role of spotter. The spotters will walk alongside the team and physically help if someone starts to lose his or her balance.
- Observe these safety guidelines: avoid stepping on each other's feet, do not participate if you have issues with your ankles, knees, or back, and be careful of the domino effect where someone loses his or her balance and falls forward, causing everyone else to topple over.

In your role as team coach, pay attention to the group dynamics that emerge during this activity. After they finish, debrief the activity using some of the discussion questions below. Be sure to share whatever observations and feedback you may have that will benefit the team.

Variations
- Get off to an easy start by having people do this in teams of two. After they make it across, combine them into teams of four people, followed by teams of eight. It's possible to form even larger teams, but the activity becomes quite a bit harder once you go beyond twelve people.
- Have the team brainstorm four to six real-life obstacles that team members must overcome on the way to the goal they identified. Before they play the game, have team members write each obstacle on a sheet of paper, then place them on the floor along the path to the finish line. Tell team members they must ski around each obstacle slalom-style on the way to the goal.

Discussion Questions
1. What was challenging about this activity?
2. Did your team come up with a strategy that helped you succeed?
3. What types of roles did people play?
4. Did you assign a leader, or did a leader emerge during the activity?
5. Was it important to have a leader?
6. How would you describe the team's communication during this activity?
7. Did the team experience any setbacks along the way? If so, how did the team respond?
8. What lessons can your team learn from this activity that you can apply to real life?

What Gets in the Way?

To focus on the accountability needed to achieve results

OBJECTIVES
- To bring awareness to the team's need for greater accountability
- To show that everyone has roadblocks that can be overcome

Group Size

Any

Materials

File folders, materials people have on hand
(e.g., cell phones, pads of paper, pens, sticky
notes, pictures of family, laptops, iPods)

Time

20 minutes

Setting the Context

Every day, people have to choose what to do with their time. It is easy to get distracted and pulled away from what is truly important and essential to reach one's goals. Things come up, such as unexpected phone calls, emails, and day-to-day details clamoring for attention. While we have good intentions of completing our "to do" list, it seems that something always gets in the way. This activity is a way to become aware of distractions and gain more control of the day.

Preparation

Gather supplies for the activity on a table, encouraging participants to contribute their personal items to the mix.

Procedure

Divide the group into teams of three. When everyone is in a triad, say, "Every day people have to choose what to do with their time and there are many competing priorities. We often make commitments with good intentions of executing them and then 'something happens.' This is a fun activity to look at what gets in the way."

Invite one person from each team to come to the main table with the props and choose the one that most represents what gets in his or her way of getting things done. That person will then return to the team and use the prop to demonstrate what causes him or her to get behind or miss important deadlines. The other two team members will then each offer suggestions for two minutes of ideas that might help the first person. The person who shared says "Thank you" and can then choose to implement any of the shared ideas or not when they get back to work. When the first person is finished, he or she hands the item to the second person, who returns it to the table as he or she chooses an item to describe his or her competing priority or procrastination challenge. Repeat as above for the second and third person.

When done, redistribute the items back to the rightful owners.

Rules

- Everyone chooses an item.
- Everyone shares what gets in their way and listens to ideas from their teammates.

Discussion Questions

1. What are some of the common challenges and distractions you face?

2. What can you collectively do about them?

3. How can you hold each other accountable?

Who, Me?

WHEN TO USE THIS GAME

When you want to reinforce the importance of accountability

OBJECTIVES
- To help people see how their actions (or lack thereof) impact others
- Have some fun

Group Size

Up to 10

Materials

Two dice, box of dominoes, cards, or Legos

Time

30 minutes

Setting the Context

When we do what we say, we move closer to achieving our organizational and team goals. This activity helps teams take a quick look at how roadblocks and excuses impact team productivity.

Preparation

Have materials available on a table.

Procedure

Have everyone take a seat around the table. Have the team take five minutes to talk about what could be built with the provided materials. What would it look like? Why is it important?

Rules

- Roll the dice. The highest number goes first, then take turns in clockwise order.
- If the person rolls an even number, he or she adds one item to the "creation."
- If the person rolls an odd number, that person must create an excuse as to why he or she can't "do the job right now."
- Continue until ten minutes have passed or the "creation" is complete, which-ever comes first.

Discussion Questions

1. What got in the way of getting the project complete?
2. What was the funniest excuse?
3. How often are excuses given instead of meeting objectives?
4. What can you do as a team to remove barriers that prevent you from being accountable?
5. What can you do as individuals to better honor your commitments?
6. How can you hold each other accountable?

8

Staying Motivated and Energized

Your talent determines what you can do. Your motivation determines how much you are willing to do. Your attitude determines how well you do it.

—Lou Holtz

Alphabet Space Trace

WHEN TO USE THIS GAME

As a fun icebreaker activity at the start of a meeting to energize the group and get everyone laughing, and as a lighthearted way to explore the differences between cooperation and competition

OBJECTIVES

- To have fun and share some laughs with the team
- To shift the team's focus from competition to cooperation

Group Size

Any, paired up with partners

Materials

None

Time

10 to 15 minutes

Setting the Context

Competition has been shown to be useful up to a certain point and no further, but cooperation, which is the thing we must strive for today, begins where competition leaves off.

—Franklin D. Roosevelt

Smart team leaders understand the delicate balance between competition and cooperation. Healthy competition can be a good thing, driving individuals to grow and push past their own limitations to achieve great results for the team. On the other hand, too much competition can lead to hurt feelings, lousy morale, diminished trust, or worse.

It's important for coaches to help teams find the sweet spot where healthy, mutually rewarding competition leads to greater cooperation and greater results. This activity can prompt some meaningful discussion about the differences between competition and cooperation.

Preparation
None

Procedure
Have team members pair up and stand face-to-face with their partner, leaving about two to three feet of space between themselves. If there is an extra person, please volunteer yourself as his or her partner. Tell the group, "When I say 'Go!', you and your partner are going to race to see who can draw the letters of the alphabet in the air between yourselves fastest. Start with the letter A and go all the way to Z, drawing the letters with your index finger. If you mess up a letter, simply redraw it and continue on. After you finish, make some noise to celebrate! Ready…Go!"

After everyone is finished, tell them, "Now let's switch gears. Instead of competing, you and your partner are going to cooperate. One of you will draw the letters of the alphabet A to Z in the air, just like before. Your partner's job will be to follow the identical path of your index finger as you draw the letters in the air. The goal is to for him or her to follow the identical path as accurately as possible. You may go as fast or as slow as you'd like. When you finish, give your partner a high five and make some noise to celebrate! Ready…Go!"

Give the group a moment to celebrate after they finish, then have them switch roles with their partners so everyone gets to be both the drawer and the follower.

Discussion Questions
1. How was this activity challenging?
2. Did you approach this activity differently when it shifted from competitive to cooperative? In what ways?
3. What did you notice when you were drawing the letters for your partner?
4. What did you notice when you were in the role of the follower?
5. What does this activity tell you about cooperation versus competition?
6. When is competition in the workplace a good thing? When is it a bad thing?
7. What is a healthy balance of competition and cooperation for your team?

Balloon Shuffle

WHEN TO USE THIS GAME

To remind team members of the importance of good communication and clear leadership, and as a great way to create team spirit and energize the group

OBJECTIVES

- To experience the whole team working in sync
- To highlight the importance of clear communication
- To illustrate the bonds that connect the team

Group Size

Any; split large groups into teams of 8 to 12

Materials

One uninflated round balloon per person, 9 inches or greater in diameter; masking tape to mark the start and finish lines

Time

15 to 20 minutes

Setting the Context

Top-performing work teams know the importance of focusing their energy toward a common goal. Just as Olympic rowing teams know that every stroke of their oars must be in perfect sync to win the race, effective work teams know that their efforts must be coordinated and streamlined to achieve their goals. This activity gives team members an experience of working in sync and highlights the importance of clear communication and leadership for the team's success.

Preparation

Mark the start and finish lines on the floor with masking tape. Place the finish line approximately thirty to forty feet from the start line. If you are in a large room or hallway, have the team move in a straight line to the finish line. If you are in a small room, have the team wind around the room to get to the finish line.

Procedure

Give each team member a balloon and have them blow it up to medium size or bigger. Have the team stand behind the start line in a single-file line, placing one balloon between each person. Everyone should move in close enough to squeeze the balloons between each other and keep them from dropping to the ground. Team members may not physically touch each other; they may only make contact with the balloons. Tell them that the object of the game is to travel together in sync all the way to the finish line, with as few dropped balloons as possible. If a balloon is dropped, the whole team must pause while the balloon is picked up and returned to its position between the people.

To boost their chance for success, have team members elect a leader to call out a cadence such as "One, two, three, left! One, two, three, right!" After they have taken several steps, have the team select a new leader. Do this several times so that multiple people get the opportunity to play a leadership role.

Variations

If you are concerned about personal space issues, try this fun option. Have the whole team line up side-to-side, squeezing the balloons between their shoulders and the shoulders of their neighbors on either side. This option requires a wide room or hallway. Have the team attempt to take ten to fifteen steps together without dropping the balloons from between anyone's shoulders.

You can add a bit of competition to this activity by having two or more teams go at once. This can sometimes result in poorer performance as more balloons are dropped in the race to the finish line.

Discussion Questions

1. Was it difficult stepping in sync with each other?

2. What role did the team leader play? Was it useful? Why or why not?

3. How would you describe your team's communication during this game?

4. What does "being in sync" mean in real life for your team?

5. Name some real-life factors that might cause your team to be out of sync?

6. What are some real-life ways to maximize the team's ability to work in sync?

7. If you had two or more teams go at once, was there a feeling of competition? What effect did competition have on the whole group's overall success?

Gravity Stick

WHEN TO USE THIS GAME

Anytime as a way to challenge teams that work well together (not for teams with internal issues or that deal poorly with conflict)

OBJECTIVES
- To work together to achieve a common goal
- To explore themes of patience, integrity, and dealing with setbacks

Group Size

6 to 14 people

Materials

A thin stick or pole 6 to 8 feet in length (e.g., a broomstick, dowel rod, bamboo stick, slender PVC pipe, cardboard tube, aluminum tent pole)

Time

20 minutes

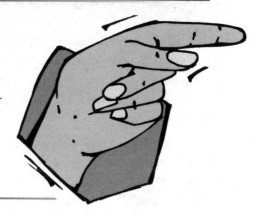

Setting the Context

A good indicator of a healthy team is how members deal with frustration or setbacks. Projects in real life may start out well, but what happens when things don't go as planned? When the going gets tough, it's up to team members to keep things positive, encourage one another with positive communication, and stay focused on the goal.

Gravity Stick is a game that seems simple at first but can quickly prove to be a tricky challenge! A high level of perseverance and patience is required for this game, so don't use it if the team has poor conflict management skills.

Preparation

None

Procedure

Have the team form two straight lines facing each other. Standing shoulder to shoulder, team members should bend their arms at the elbow and extend their index fingers as if they are pointing at the person across from them. Everyone's fingers should be held at shoulder height, creating a level platform to set the stick on. Place the stick on top of everyone's extended fingers, then tell them the goal is to lower the stick all the way to the ground. The challenge is for everyone's index fingers to constantly stay in contact with the stick. If someone's finger loses contact at any time, that person needs to immediately regain contact with the stick. Participants may not use their thumbs or other fingers during this activity.

The team may be surprised and amused by what happens on their first try. Instead of being lowered, the stick may rise up as if it is floating away! If this happens, remove the stick, give the team a few moments to regroup, then have them try again starting at shoulder level. Teams may experience the stick floating away a number of times as they work through this challenge. It may take several tries before the team comes up with a strategy that works.

Tips

- Pay close attention to the tone of the team. After several tries, some teams find that laughter and amusement have given way to frustration and impatience. Encourage team members to keep the tone light, support one another, and remember that although the task is difficult, it can be done.
- Avoid putting yourself in the position of judging whether people are keeping contact with the stick. Allowing team members to monitor themselves can result in some good discussion about integrity and accountability.
- Some teams may come up with a creative solution to this challenge, crouching or lying down to make "shoulder" height closer to the ground.

Variations

Use a Hula-Hoop instead of a stick. Have the team stand in a circle and place the hoop on top of their extended index fingers, then proceed with the directions as outlined above.

Discussion Questions

1. What was challenging about this activity?

2. How did the team respond to setbacks?

3. Did anyone feel that someone else was to blame?

4. How would you describe the team's attitude during the activity?

5. How can teams pull together when things don't go as planned?

6. What advice would you give teams trying this activity for the first time?

7. What lessons can your team learn from this activity that you can apply to real life?

Pipeline to Success

WHEN TO USE THIS GAME

As a way to challenge and energize the team, as a lead-in to a team goal-setting session, or as a way to illustrate the concept of flexibility in planning

OBJECTIVES

- To set and achieve a clearly defined team goal
- To brainstorm ways to improve a process
- To highlight the importance of planning and flexibility

Group Size

5 to 16 people

Materials

One pipeline segment per person, masking tape, tape measure, three marbles per team, three inexpensive plastic buckets or tumblers per team, a stopwatch or timer

Time

20 to 25 minutes

Setting the Context

Sooner or later, most teams find that things rarely go according to plan. Unanticipated setbacks may happen, team members may come and go, and other priorities may scream for your attention. In these situations, flexibility in planning is essential for teams. The ability to stay focused on the goal and quickly adapt to whatever roadblocks or surprises come along can make the difference between success and failure.

Preparation

To make the pipeline segments, purchase lengths of vinyl bullnose corner bead from the drywall section of your local hardware store. Bullnose is the material used in home construction to create smooth, rounded corners where walls meet. An eight-foot length of vinyl bullnose corner bead typically costs between four and five dollars. The product comes in various shapes; for this activity, choose lengths with rounded edges that a marble can easily roll through. Use sharp scissors to cut the bullnose edging into segments of eighteen inches each.

Mark a start line on the ground with a piece of masking tape. Place one of the buckets or tumblers one foot from the start line, place the second bucket or tumbler twelve feet from the start line, and place the third bucket or tumbler about thirty feet from the start line.

Procedure

Give each participant one pipeline segment. Tell the team that the object is for everyone to line up their segments end-to-end and roll a marble through the pipeline, depositing it into a bucket at the end. There will be three buckets set up. One is really close to the starting line, one is about twelve feet away, and one is really far (about thirty feet away). Once they get a marble into a bucket, they need to move on to a new bucket. At the end, they will have gotten one marble into each of the three buckets. They must follow these rules:

Rules

- All marbles must be initiated from behind the start line.
- A marble must be deposited into each bucket by rolling it through everyone's pipe.
- Marbles must roll all the way through everyone's pipe.
- Your hands can't touch someone else's pipe.
- When a marble is in your pipe, you can't move your feet. Otherwise move your feet all you want.
- If a marble gets dropped, the team has to start over again.
- Have the team practice, allowing them up to ten minutes to create a strategy and work out roles for everyone. After they have practiced, tell the team to set a time goal that will be "challenging but doable." The clock will start when you say Go! and stop when the team gets the third marble into the third bucket. Give the team several attempts to achieve their goal. Once they achieve their goal, have the team come up with a new goal that will really challenge them, for example, shaving 25 percent off their time.

Discussion Questions

1. How did this activity challenge the team?

2. Was the goal clear to everyone?

3. How did changing to a new, more difficult goal affect the team?

4. What did the team do when a marble was dropped? In other words, how did the team deal with setbacks?

5. How would you describe the team in terms of flexibility?

Team Story Time Line

WHEN TO USE THIS GAME

For teams that have worked together for a while, when the team has reached an important milestone, or when the team is starting a new project

OBJECTIVES

- To recognize and celebrate the team's past achievements
- To draw lessons from the past that will make the team even better in the future
- To gain an understanding of the team's strengths and challenges

Group Size

Up to 16

Materials

A large whiteboard with dry-erase markers or several sheets of flip-chart paper, masking tape, markers

Time

30 to 45 minutes

Setting the Context

Beginnings and endings of projects provide great opportunities for teams to take stock of where they've been. By reflecting on the successes and challenges they have faced together, team members can gain important insights that will help them be even more effective in the future.

Preparation

Arrange the room with the chairs facing the whiteboard or flip-chart pages. If you are using flip-chart paper, tape the sheets next to each other end to end in landscape orientation along the wall.

Procedure

Tell the group that they will be working together to create a visual history of the team called a Team Story Time Line. Each person will contribute by adding his or her own drawings, doodles, and written words to illustrate the highs, lows, successes, and challenges that have brought the team to where they are today.

1. Have the group choose a starting point for their Team Story Time Line. The starting point can be when the team was formed, when they started on their project, or even as far back as when the company began. Tell them to indicate their starting point on the far left side of the time line in a creative way, using a drawing, doodle, or written words.

2. The opposite end of their time line represents now, the present. Have the team indicate this on the far right side of their time line using drawings, doodles, words, or simply today's date.

3. Now that they have the starting and end points, it's up to the team to fill in the rest of their story. Ask them to think about the elements that are a part of their collective history: the people, the challenges, the goals, the successes, the setbacks, and the important decisions that have taken them from their starting point all the way to the present day. Invite all the team members to add something to the time line that helps tell their story.

4. Encourage creativity! Drawings, sketches, doodles, caricatures, and stick figures can bring the Team Story Time Line to life. Written words are okay too but should be used sparingly.

5. Team Story Time Line should include some or all of the following categories:
   - **People and Staff.** Have team members add themselves to the time line based on when they joined the team. If the team has a lot of people, it's a good idea to write the name of each person next to his or her drawing. They can also include former team members on the time line, especially if they played an important role for the team.

- **Important Decisions** that have made an impact on the team. A fork in the road is a good way to symbolize decision points, but the team may have even better ways to represent their important decisions. Add some text to the drawing to make it clear, if necessary.
- **Obstacles or Barriers** that challenged the team. What kinds of obstacles has the team faced? Tight deadlines, tough competitors, a lousy economy, or internal issues can truly challenge teams. One team we worked with used doodles of Godzilla, King Kong, Bigfoot, and the Loch Ness Monster, labeled with the names of their major competitors, to represent their obstacles. Be creative!
- **Important Milestones** reached by the team or by individual team members. These can include goals reached, deadlines met, new clients won, and breakthroughs and innovations for the team.
- **Memorable Moments** that are a part of the team's history. Many of these will be work-related, but don't forget moments like holiday parties, off-site team-building events, volunteer work the team may have been involved with, or other moments that happened away from the office.
- **Important Awards and Recognitions** earned by the team or by individual team members, such as industry awards, individual professional certifications earned, or educational achievements and degrees earned.

6. Be sure to conclude this activity with some of the discussion questions below. Creating a Team Story Time Line is a great way for the team to learn from their past and set the stage for greater successes in the future.

Tips

Encourage greater participation by moving everyone's chairs closer to the time line.

Take digital photos of the finished Team Story Time Line and email them to everyone. If the team created their Team Story Time Line on flip-chart paper, have them hang it someplace where it's visible around the office.

Discussion Questions

1. What moments are you most proud of?

2. What is the most significant moment on the time line for you as an individual? (Invite team members to share them one at a time if they wish.)

3. What is something meaningful that each person has brought to the team? (Invite team members to share aloud the names of individuals along with an expression of thanks, recognition, or appreciation.)

4. What obstacles have you struggled with the most in the past? What are some strategies that can help you overcome similar obstacles in the future?

5. What skills, knowledge, expertise, or awareness can you add to the team to make you more effective in the future?

6. If you had a magic wand that allowed you to change three things from the past, what would they be? Why?

7. What are the most important lessons you have learned from the past?

Transport

WHEN TO USE THIS GAME

With a team that is in the performing stage of group development, or with a team that is in the storming stage

OBJECTIVES

- To foster creative problem solving
- To experience full-team commitment to a goal

Group Size

6 to 15

Materials

Blue painter's tape, one bowling ball, 8 segments of rope that are each 8 feet long, tape measure

Time

20 to 30 minutes

Setting the Context

Because of the difficulty level of this game, it works best with a team that is in the performing stage of group development. Another option is to use the game in the storming stage to incite conflict within the team. This is more delicate and challenging to facilitate effectively but allows for some excellent coaching opportunities.

Preparation

Using the blue painter's tape, create a four-foot square on the floor. Take two short lengths of tape and create an *X* in the center of the square. Place the bowling ball on the *X*. Take two additional lengths of tape and create another *X* on the ground about three feet from the outside of the four-foot box (the farther away you put this second *X*, the harder you make it for the team). Place the eight-foot ropes next to the square.

Procedure

Using only the eight ropes, the team needs to construct a device to transport the bowling ball from the center of the square to the new location marked by the *X* on the outside of the square. The team must formulate a plan and work in perfect unison to accomplish their goal.

Rules

- Every team member must be involved in executing the plan.
- All team members must remain outside the square.
- No part of any team member's body can cross the plane of the square. No hands, arms, heads, or noses.
- No knots can be tied in the ropes.
- Only the ropes can contact the ball.
- If the ball is dropped, it needs to be reset on the X in the center of the square.

The team will quickly get to work, each person grabbing a rope and individually trying to loop it around the ball. Remind them of the rules, as this solution forces them to break the rules because their arms and hands cross the plane of the square. In addition, it doesn't work because it doesn't build a solid structure for the ball. You don't have to mention that it won't work but rather remind them that they are breaking the rules. Oftentimes, teams will ignore the facilitator/coach as they try "really hard" to make this solution work. If this occurs, you can address it in the debriefing discussion, or if a team is getting frustrated, stop the game and facilitate a mid-activity brief discussion with your team.

A good solution and one that complies with the rules is for the team to create a net outside the square, strategically move the net over the square and lower the net under the ball, being careful to keep all body parts outside the square. The team then needs to pull the ropes together to secure the ball so that it can be lifted and carried to the destination. This is much easier said than done, because a team may have a great solution but lack the patience and team coordination to carry it out successfully. As the coach, be prepared to step in and offer feedback and insight to motivate them to continue their task.

Coach Notes: As team coach, take some time to consider how you will design the structure of the game. It's good to base your decisions on your team's level of skill, their stage of group formation, and your goals for the team. Here are some things to consider beforehand:

- Think about how much distance you want between the ball and its destination. The farther the ball is from the destination, the more difficult the challenge.
- Does a dropped ball indicate a setback or a failure? From what height? Most groups will drop the ball several times as they develop their plan. You may decide that it's part of the process, or you may want to stop the game for a quick check-in. Either way, it's good to have an answer ready when the team looks to you for guidance as they "fail forward."

- How closely will you monitor and enforce the rules? Will you ask the group to monitor themselves and inform you, or will you keep a watchful eye? Is there a penalty for breaking the rules? What is the penalty for breaking the rules?

Discussion Questions

1. What was your level of motivation throughout the activity? Did it change? What caused it to change? How did you overcome lack of interest or motivation?
2. In what way did that impact your experience?
3. What was necessary for a successful completion of this challenge?
4. What did it feel like to have the entire team completely committed to the goal?
5. In what ways can you apply this to your daily work?
6. How would you prefer to receive feedback when you get off track?

9

Celebrating Success

A great coach is measured by the success of others.

—Edward E. Scannell

A Real Knee-Slapper

WHEN TO USE THIS GAME
At the end of a meeting or work session

OBJECTIVES
- To have fun and bond with your teammates
- To experience a quick team challenge

Group Size
  6 to 20
Materials
  A chair for each person
Time
  5 to 10 minutes

Setting the Context
It's important to celebrate after any success, big or small. Getting in the habit of acknowledging a job well done may not come naturally for some teams, but it is important for a team to adopt that habit. A coach can help remind the team how important this is and how it can do wonders for team morale.

Preparation
None

Procedure
Arrange the chairs in a tight circle so everyone is seated close to one another. Include yourself in the circle. Say to the group:

"One of the things I like most about going to sports events is the energy of the crowd. I'm sure most of you are familiar with the Wave, where people in the crowd jump up, throw their hands in the air, and make lots of noise as they try to make the Wave go all the way around the arena. For this activity, we will be attempting a variation called the Knee-Slap Wave.

1. Place your hands on your knees, with your left hand on your left knee and your right hand on your right knee.
2. Raise your hands so that they are floating a few inches directly above your knees.
3. Move your hands slowly outward, with your left hand moving to the left and your right hand moving to the right, until they are floating above the knees of the people sitting to your left and right.
4. Now lower your hands onto the knees of your neighbors.

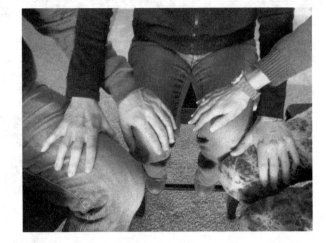

"With our arms criss-crossed like this, we are now ready to attempt a Knee-Slap Wave. The object is to pass a knee-slap in perfect sequential order all the way around our circle until it comes back to where it started. I will start our Wave by slapping this knee. [Wiggle your fingers or wave your hand so everyone can see which knee you are talking about.] Whoever's hand is on the next knee down the line should slap it, followed by the next knee, and so on. Because our arms are criss-crossed, you will have to pay pretty close attention to get it right! If anyone messes up, we'll have to try again. Here we go!"

After the team is successful, be sure to celebrate with some cheers and applause!

Tips

- This activity is a little tricky but easily doable after a few tries. Teams that go slow do best.
- If the team is making a lot of mistakes, encourage them to think before they slap!

Count on Me

WHEN TO USE THIS GAME

When you want everyone to deepen their appreciation of the
strengths and talents of other team members

OBJECTIVES

- To notice how effectively team members operate when focusing
  on their strengths
- To develop appreciation for one's own talents and skills and those
  of team members

Group Size

Any

Materials

Name tags, large poster boards of various colors,
balloons, glitter, markers, ribbon, tape, anything else
you think would be fun

Time

30 to 40 minutes

Setting the Context

Team members often go about their jobs
without paying attention or appreciating
the roles others play. With this activity, the
team takes on a fun project where everyone
gets to play the role that most closely aligns with their strengths.

Preparation

Have enough supplies for the number of teams formed. Place all the supplies on one table.

Determine what roles might be needed, i.e., Creator, Project Manager,
Designer, Doer, Quality Control, Facilitator (you can adapt these role
names to fit your organization's preferred titles). Write the names of the

roles on the name tags, assigning one role for each name tag. Make sure you have enough name tags so every team member will have one.

Procedure

Ask the teams to think about the roles they usually play on the team or on projects. Say, "For this activity I'd like you to choose the role that feels closest to your normal role. The roles are: Creator, Project Manager, Designer, Doer, Quality Control, and Facilitator. Take the name tag of the role you will play. Introduce yourself to the group with your new role."

Tell them they will be creating a tribute to the team using the supplies available and that they will have twenty minutes. The tribute can be anything they choose. Invite the Creator and Project Manager from each table to come up and choose the supplies for their team. Once each team has supplies, each person contributes to the effort while playing his or her role. Announce time at ten minutes and five minutes remaining. Walk around providing encouragement. When the teams have completed their tributes, ask the Facilitator for each team to show off their creation and add any explanations or descriptions. Ask them to hang their creation on the wall.

Rules

- Everyone contributes to the success of the endeavor.
- The tributes can be anything the team wants.

Discussion Questions

1. What did you notice about how the teams achieved the goal?
2. What do you want to acknowledge your team members for?
3. What are your collective strengths?
4. What skills might your team want to develop?
5. What was challenging?
6. What might you like more of or less of in your job or team role?
7. What learning from this can you apply to the team going forward?

Coach Note: A variation could be to ask each person to choose the role that is least like them for this activity. If they are not sure, ask them to get input from their teammates so everyone chooses a role that is a bit of a stretch.

Kudos to You

WHEN TO USE THIS GAME

To provide energy during challenging times, to reset the team after a failure, or to bring closure at the end of a project

OBJECTIVES

- To build motivation and self-confidence of team members
- To provide appreciation for the contribution of others on the team

Group Size

Up to 20

Materials

Paper and pens (cardstock is preferred), one standard letter-sized mailing envelope for each person

Time

20 to 30 minutes

Setting the Context

We each bring our unique personality, talents, and strengths to a team. Providing a framework for team members to acknowledge the contributions of others helps to build a healthy, interdependent team. This easy activity is the perfect takeaway to indicate the significance of the relationships between team members, the difference team members make to one another, and the specific ways others have contributed to the success of the team.

It is also a great way for team members to understand and acknowledge the contributions they make to the team. When you hear about your strengths from others and acknowledge them yourself, this builds individual motivation and self-confidence.

Preparation

None

Procedure

Ask team members to arrange their chairs in a circle and take a seat. You, as coach, are encouraged to participate, because the team will look to show their appreciation for your role on the team. Start with a discussion about the value of positive feedback. Ask these questions:

- What is the value of positive feedback?
- What makes it meaningful?
- In what ways does it influence the energy of a team?

Tell the team that they will have the opportunity to acknowledge the contributions of everyone in the circle. Pass out one piece of paper and a pen to each team member. Follow these steps for the activity:

- Ask each participant to write his or her own name legibly on the bottom of the paper. (**Coach Note:** It's important that his or her name is at the bottom of the page.)
- Have participants pass their paper to the person to their left.
- That person writes one word, two words, or even a few sentences, *at the top* of the page, to describe what he or she has valued about the person whose name is written on the bottom of the paper. Ask team members to take a moment to reflect before writing on the page.
- When they are finished writing, instruct them to fold the paper neatly so the comments are covered.
- Pass the paper to the next person and follow the same process until each person receives his or her original paper.
- Invite team members to unfold their pages and read the comments quietly.
- Ask each person to identify one particularly meaningful comment that was written on his or her page.
- Invite team members to stand up shoulder to shoulder and, one at a time, say the meaningful message aloud using the words "I am…" or "I have…"
- Provide an envelope to each person for safekeeping of his or her feedback.

Discussion Questions

1. How often do you take time to acknowledge the positive contributions of your teammates?
2. How often do you take time to acknowledge your own strengths?
3. Why is it important to take time for activities such as this?
4. What are other "things like this" that you can do to acknowledge one another?

We Rock

To build team confidence and/or morale

OBJECTIVES
- To reflect on past successes
- To create a sense of unity

Group Size

Any

Materials

Rock, cell phone, glue stick, playing cards, keys, eyeglasses, sunglasses, suntan lotion, candy, paper clips, staples, rubber bands, tape, nail, hammer, construction paper, crayons and/or markers, sticky notes, any other creative supplies

Time

20 to 40 minutes, depending on group size

Setting the Context

Let's look back and reflect on our many awesome accomplishments. This is a time to acknowledge the team and each other for our achievements.

Preparation

Put the supplies on a table.

Procedure

Ask each person to look over the supplies and think about how one of the items is a reminder of a past team success or the strength someone else on the team possesses. People are welcome to draw (or talk about) any item not physically present. Each person takes one item (no duplication) and everyone has two to three minutes to think about a story from the team's history they want to share. Remove any item not chosen. After everyone shares, celebrate with a team huddle, pile hands in the center and shout, "We rock!"

For fun, you may want to take a group picture with the items, to remind the team of their many talents and achievements.

Rules

- Everyone chooses an item.
- Have each person share a story and relate how the item chosen reminds him or her of the story.
- After each person shares, the item is placed at the center of the table.

Discussion Questions

1. What did you learn about your team?

2. What fond memory had you forgotten?

3. When are you at your best?

4. How do your combined strengths make the team stronger?

5. What strengths do you need to tap into going forward?

10

Transforming the Team

The coach is not the problem solver. In sports, I had to learn how to teach less, so that more could be learned. The same holds true for a coach in business.

—W. Timothy Gallwey

Six-Count Sequence

To reenergize the team, increase engagement during meetings or when the team is ready to develop a culture of coaching

OBJECTIVES
- To master a simple but difficult challenge
- To let team members practice coaching each other

Group Size

Any; split large groups into teams of 3 to 4

Materials

None

Time

15 minutes

Setting the Context

This game sets the stage for the team to develop a culture of peer coaching. It gives team members the opportunity to help and coach each other toward mastery of a challenging task and clearly illustrates the way coaching benefits the team.

Preparation

Allow plenty of time to learn and practice the combined six-count sequence yourself. Do this prior to the meeting, because you will need to demonstrate it several times.

Procedure

Tell the team they will be counting from one to six. The challenge is there is a different arm position for every number of the six-count. For each number of your count, you will be raising and lowering your right arm one way, while raising and lowering your left arm in a completely different way. Raise and lower your arms like when you do jumping jacks. It helps to learn the motion for each arm independently, then combine them after you have gained competency. Here are the motions:

Left Arm (raise and lower like a jumping jack):

1. Raise it all the way up in the air.
2. Lower it all the way back down to your side.
3. Raise it all the way back up.
4. Lower it all the way back down.
5. Raise it all the way back up.
6. Lower it all the way back down.

Right Arm (raise and lower like a jumping jack):

1. Raise it all the way up in the air.
2. Lower it halfway (to horizontal position).
3. Lower it all the way back down to your side.
4. Raise it all the way up in the air.
5. Lower it halfway (to horizontal position).
6. Lower it all the way back down to your side.

Demonstrate the motion of each arm one at a time for the whole group. Invite them to join along and practice with you a few times. Keep in mind that if you are facing the group, left and right will be reversed!

After they have practiced each arm, demonstrate what it looks like with both arms combined. Go slowly and have them try to follow along as you demonstrate a few times. Then say to the group:

"In order for you to become expert counters, I invite you to gather into teams of three or four. Take about seven minutes in your teams to coach and help each other learn the combined six-count sequence until everyone has gained competency. Good luck!"

After seven minutes, invite everyone to join you once again as you do the combined six-count sequence. Finish with a big round of applause to celebrate everyone's hard work!

Tips

Circulate among the teams as they practice the combined six-count movements, answering any questions they may have.

Discussion Questions

1. What was difficult about this activity?
2. Did you notice any improvement?
3. How did it help to receive coaching from your teammates?
4. Were you open to coaching?
5. Was there a certain coaching style that helped you most?
6. What are some real-life ways you can help and provide coaching for each other?
7. What can you do to be open to coaching and help from one another?

Blindfold Maze Crossing

When you would like to deepen the trust on the team

OBJECTIVES
- To experience the coaching relationship
- To build and practice coaching skills

Group Size

Up to 20

Materials

Masking tape or rope, assorted objects,
blindfolds (optional)

Time

30 to 40 minutes

Setting the Context

Coaching is an attitude first and a skill set second. Allowing your team to experience what it feels like to coach and be coached can be a rich learning experience. In this activity, team members learn while doing, which also increases their coaching proficiency at a faster pace.

Preparation

Using masking tape or a long rope, section off a large rectangle on the ground (ten by twenty feet is about the right size). Scatter objects throughout the inside of the rectangular playing area, placing the items about one foot apart from each other. Objects can be flat foam shapes found at your local craft store, crumpled-up paper from the recycling bin, or whatever props you have handy. Asking team members to bring assorted props (staplers, folders, sticky pads) for the game gets them involved from the start. You can use blindfolds or you can instruct them on "coachee body language," which is using one hand to cover their eyes and using the other hand "bumpers up," out in front of them to create a safety zone that prevents them from bumping into other sightless coachees they may encounter while navigating through the area.

Procedure

Have the team form partnerships. Each person will play the role of coach and coachee during the activity. Explain that while acting as coachee, each person will have to travel from one side of the rectangle to the other without stepping on any of the objects. The challenge is that they will have to do this without the use of their eyes. Instead, their personal coach will direct them safely through the area, using verbal commands only. If an object is touched, bumped, or stepped on, the coachee will have to start again. Usually these "do-overs" result in better communication between coach and coachee as they learn from experience what works and what does not. As facilitator, you can be as loose or strict with the rules as you choose, impacting the difficulty of the activity. Adhering closely to the rules and having them begin over for any brush with an object allows them to practice creating a dialogue that works for both of them. Explain the rules this way:

Rules

- Each person will get to play the role of coach and coachee.
- While in the role of coachee, you will have to travel across the area without touching any of the objects, while blindfolded [using a blindfold or their hands to cover their eyes].
- While coaching, you will have to guide the person using only verbal communication—that is, without physically touching your coachee.
- If an object is touched, the coachee begins again.
- Once the coachee is safely across, switch roles.
- Before the second person begins, you may choose to take a few minutes to discuss what worked and what didn't to increase the efficacy of your coaching.

Discussion Questions

1. How did your coach's attitude influence your experience?

2. In what way did that impact your success?

3. When you were coach, what skills did you use to guide your coachee?

4. In what ways is coaching a partnership?

5. What is needed from the coach and the coachee for a successful outcome?

6. What will you commit to so that you can become a team of coaches?

7. How can you hold each other accountable?

Concentric Coaching

WHEN TO USE THIS GAME

To give people a chance to get to know one another and to use coaching questions

Group Size

Any; split large group into teams of 10 to 12

Materials

Timer, bell, or gong, Concentric Coaching Questions handout

Time

20 to 30 minutes

Setting the Context

One of the most important tools a coach uses is asking powerful questions. Sometimes coaches don't even know what the topic is, but asking a thoughtful question can assist a colleague or employee in reaching a breakthrough solution.

Preparation

Make copies of the Concentric Coaching Questions on the last page of this activity. Create enough for half of the participants to have a copy. If you want to give everyone a chance to play both roles, double the amount of time for the activity.

Procedure

Have the team form two circles of five or six people each, one inside the other. The inside circle faces out; the outside circle faces in. Position the circles so each person is sitting or standing face-to-face with someone in the other circle. If you have an odd number, be prepared to join in. If there are more than ten or twelve people, form more circles. Inform them that they will be on the move during this activity. Let them know the inner circle will be the coaches and the outer circle will receive coaching as coachees. Tell the outer circle (the coachees) to think of something personal or professional that they would be willing to share that they could use some clarity on. Examples could include how to focus on a fitness goal, better time management, better interpersonal skills, and so on. They will start with one coach and then each minute will move to another coach. While the coach changes, the coachee will keep the same topic and the next coach will ask another question to drive deeper into the heart of the subject until it's time to move on.

While the coachees are thinking of a topic, call a huddle of the coaches. Give them the list of questions (photocopied from the last page of this activity). Tell them that they should ask the first person the first question and then listen deeply to the response. Based on what they hear, they should continue to ask powerful, open-ended questions to help the person gain clarity. When the minute is up, use a bell, gong or yell out, "Time to move on," and instruct them how they will be moving (for example, "Outside circle, move one person to your left," or "Inside circle, move one person to your right) so that every time they move they have a new partner). Once everyone has a new partner, start the next round of conversations with the next question. The coaches will then continue to ask questions based on the response. It is not their job to give advice or solutions, only to ask questions that help the coachee create his or her own solution. After the first round, the coach may not even know what the topic truly is. If they are asking good, thoughtful questions, the coachee will figure out a solution without having to divulge information that satisfies the coaches' curiosity but does not help the coachee.

After each round and before moving on, make sure they give their partner some form of a thank-you—a pat on the back, a high five, a verbal "Thanks for the conversation" or some other form of appreciation—get creative!

Rules

1. One group of participants rotates each minute, the other remains stationary.

2. The inner circle participants are the coaches. They can only ask questions, not offer advice or solutions.

3. The coach will start with the first question on the provided list and then ask any other open-ended question(s) that seem appropriate based on the conversation.

4. The outer circle, or coachees, will choose an issue they wish to work on and will continue to work on it with each of the coaches.

5. The content that is shared during this activity remains confidential. The lessons learned can be debriefed without sharing content. The only person who can share confidential info is the person who is impacted by it. For example, a coachee could say, "I had a breakthrough on _____ because of this coaching experience and I want to commit to this new behavior."

Discussion Questions

1. Coachees, how did it feel to divulge personal information?

2. Coaches, how did it feel to only ask questions and not offer advice?

3. How does an activity like this build trust within the team?

4. What are some other ways you can use powerful questions on your team?

5. What are some other ways you can build a trusting team?

6. How can your team be more coach-like with each other?

Concentric Coaching Questions

- What would you like to focus on? What is important about that to you?

- If you could have this work out just the way you want, what would that give you?

- What challenges might get in your way?

- What tools or skills do you have to enable you to achieve your goal?

- What else do you need to think through?

- What excites you most about attaining this goal? How will you celebrate your success?

Feedforward for Success

WHEN TO USE THIS GAME

When team members trust each other enough to ask for help and share ideas freely

OBJECTIVES

- To get team members to ask for help on something that is important to them
- To get team members to offer their ideas without being attached to their implementation

Group Size

Any

Materials

Paper and pens

Time

20 minutes

Setting the Context

The purpose of the Marshall Goldsmith feedforward technique is to help team members achieve a positive change in the behaviors they select by providing the team members with suggestions they can implement now and in the future. Instead of rehashing a past that cannot be changed using feedback, Jon Katzenbach (author of *The Wisdom of Teams*) and Marshall Goldsmith coined "feedforward" to encourage spending time creating a future.

You can change the future. You can't change the past. Athletes are often coached using feedforward. Basketball players are taught to imagine the basketball going in the hoop and to visualize the perfect dunk shot. By giving you ideas on how you can be even more successful, feedforward will increase your likelihood of achieving this success.

Preparation

Clear adequate floor space for everyone to comfortably be able to move around the room. Push in chairs and remove purses or other items that could be tripped on. You can also conduct this activity in a lobby area or outside for a change of scenery.

Procedure

Ask each person to think for a minute or two and write down several ideas about something they would like to improve upon. It could be a specific behavior or the ability to accomplish a task more effectively. Examples include "I would like to be a better communicator" or "I would like to improve my time-management skills." Tell them they will be asking their colleagues for input on this topic. Then ask them to circle the one they would most like to focus on for this activity. Say, "You will now have ten minutes to circulate around the room. Approach another person and greet him or her. Ask the other person what he or she wants to improve. Listen and offer several suggestions based on your knowledge and experience."

The person receiving the ideas should only say, "Thank you." The person receiving the ideas does not commit to using the idea, does not say whether he or she has already tried the idea, and does not say it's a bad idea—just "Thank you." Then have partners switch roles and repeat the process. Each person should have about one minute to share.

When the pair's first conversation ends, have them find new partners. Continue to repeat the process until time is called. Encourage everyone to return to their chairs and take five minutes to jot down the ideas they think would be most beneficial and begin to think about how and when they could implement the idea. Then begin the debriefing with the discussion questions.

Rules

- Everyone comes up with one idea they want help on and sticks with it for the duration of the activity.
- Everyone freely offers whatever helpful suggestions they can.
- Everyone remains unattached to the ideas they have offered; there are no hard feelings if suggestions are not implemented.
- There is no discussion of the ideas, no back talk, only "Thank you."
- Clarifying questions are permitted to more fully understand an idea.

Discussion Questions

1. What did you like about this exercise?
2. How did it feel to ask for help?
3. How did it feel to offer help freely?
4. Does anyone want to share what they were working on and a suggestion they plan to implement?
5. How can you use this Feedforward for Success activity in the future?

Grid Walk

WHEN TO USE THIS GAME

When team members are reluctant to make decisions, make mistakes, or try new things

OBJECTIVES

- To practice in-the-moment peer coaching
- To demonstrate how making mistakes can contribute to team growth

Group Size

Up to 20

Materials

Blue painter's tape or masking tape, tape measure, grid maps, a pen, five items to use as markers (such as large sticky notes, paper plates, Beanie Babies); a dog-training clicker is optional

Time

30 to 40 minutes

Setting the Context

In the course of working together, teams sometimes experience periods of stagnation or of being "stuck." Status quo is not getting them where they need to be, but there is a reluctance to try new things for fear of making mistakes. In this game, everyone experiences making mistakes and helping prevent other team members from making the same mistakes. Team members can see firsthand how mistakes made in a supportive environment can contribute to goal achievement, and how if a team is open with mistakes, they can create a learning experience for the entire team. In addition, when the team creates a culture that allows for openly communicating mistakes, it contributes to a higher level of trust on the team.

Preparation

A large empty space is needed for this activity. Using blue painter's tape or masking tape, create the grid on the floor. Two team members working together is the most efficient way to create the grid. The grid is nine squares by six squares. Each square needs to be about eighteen inches on each side to be large enough for team members to stand in with both feet. Copy one of the grid maps provided at the end of this activity for the facilitator to use during the game. The facilitator will use the grid map to track team member's moves as they proceed through the grid. Maps are for the facilitator only; make sure the team members cannot see the map during the activity. An easy way to track this is to put a slash (/) on any incorrect square that has been stepped on. If someone steps on the same incorrect square again, place a slash is the other direction (\), making an "X". Slashes are "good moves" because they forward the progression; "X's" are "bad moves" because they indicate where the team did not learn from their mistakes. Place the five markers next to the grid in a visible location. These indicate the team's learning. When a marker is removed, it indicates a time when the team did not learn from their previous mistake.

Procedure

The task is for the team to find the correct pathway through the grid. Say to the team:

"Your challenge is to find the one right pathway that will get you safely through the grid. To do that requires discovering what doesn't work. There is no penalty for the process of discovery, but if you re-create any missteps, you will be penalized. We will track penalties with these five markers. Before beginning, you will have time to establish a plan if you choose to do so."

Then read the rules to participants:

Rules

- Only one person may be on the grid at a time.
- The path is contiguous. There is no jumping or skipping over spaces on the grid.
- Each person may continue until he or she hits a bad square, then he or she must exit the grid and let the next teammate take his or her turn.

- If a team member steps on an incorrect square, he or she will get "clicked," which indicates that person has to exit the grid.
- There is no penalty for stepping on a bad square the first time. However, each time a bad square is stepped on again, one of your markers is taken away.
- The team must establish a set rotation for traversing the grid.
- You cannot use paper to diagram the path or track progress by marking the grid in any way.
- The rest of the team may offer assistance to the person on the grid but has to do so without touching the grid at any time.

After they find the correct pathway, you may choose to have the entire team follow each other through the maze, which is the only time multiple team members are allowed on the grid.

Discussion Questions

1. What was your experience being out on the grid alone?
2. What was the penalty for stepping on an incorrect square? What are the reasons you may have hesitated choosing a square?
3. When you were on the grid, what did your teammates do to help or hinder your progress?
4. How well did you provide coaching or assistance to your teammates? What could you have done differently?
5. Did the team have a strategy for coaching those who were on the grid? How well did you follow that strategy?
6. What are the lessons learned from this game?
7. In what ways can you use the lessons learned to improve the way you get your work done?

Grid Maps

Grid Map #1

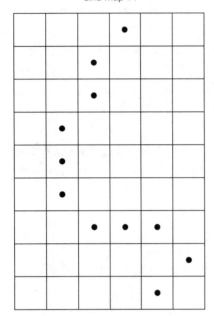

Grid Map #2

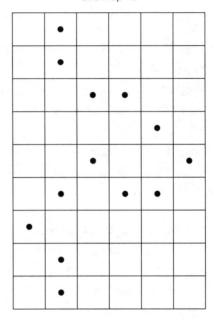

Grid Map #3

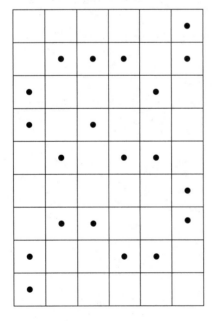

What's on the Inside?

WHEN TO USE THIS GAME

In the transforming stage, to create a space for team members to reflect on the skills they can tap into to be an effective peer coach

OBJECTIVES

To align team members' natural abilities to effective coaching

To build coaching action plan skills

Group Size

Up to 20

Materials

Flip-chart paper, markers, writing paper, pens

Time

20 to 30 minutes

AGH

BECOMING
AT ONE
WITH YOUR WORK

Setting the Context

Creating a supportive and encouraging team of peer coaches will ultimately transform the team. This process can be accelerated when team members realize the coaching skills they already possess.

Preparation

Post one blank flip-chart page for brainstorming. Pass out paper and pens to the team members.

Procedure

1. Have the group brainstorm the characteristics and qualities that make an ideal peer coach. As the group brainstorms, record all ideas on the flip-chart page. Allow five to seven minutes for brainstorming.

2. Ask team members to draw the outline of a person on their paper.

3. On the inside of their person, participants write down words from the brainstorming session they believe describe their individual peer-coaching style.
4. Ask each team member to share their words and drawings with the rest of the group.
5. After a person has finished sharing, invite other team members to suggest additional characteristics based on what they see in that person.
6. The last part of this activity is an individual step. Have participants write a personal action plan on how they could better coach and support others on the team using the skills and abilities they identified. Allow five minutes for silent reflection and writing.

Discussion Questions

1. How well did your individual attributes match the team's brainstormed ideas?
2. What did you discover about yourself?
3. Each of you now has a personal action plan. In what ways can the team support your plan?
4. What can you do on an ongoing basis to ensure you support each other's action plans?

Sources

Blanchard, Ken, Susan Fowler, and Laurence Hawkins. 2005. *Self Leadership and the One Minute Manager: Increasing Effectiveness Through Situational Self Leadership.* New York: William Morrow.

Duke Corporate Education 2006. *Coaching and Feedback for Performance.* Chicago: Dearborn Trade Publishing.

Gerzon, Mark. 2006. *Leading Through Conflict: How Successful Leaders Transform Differences into Opportunities.* Boston: Harvard Business School Press.

Goldsmith, Marshall. 2002. "Try Feedforward Instead of Feedback."

Adapted from *Leader to Leader.* Rancho Sante Fe, CA: Marshall Goldsmith Library, http://www.marshallgoldsmithlibrary.com/cim/articles_display.php?aid=110

Group & Organization Studies (pre-1986) 2 (4): 419–27, http://www.freewebs.com/group-management/BruceTuckman(1).pdf

International Coach Federation website, www.CoachFederation.org

Katzenbach, Jon R., and Douglas K. Smith. 2003. *The Wisdom of Teams.* New York: HarperCollins.

Millbower, Lenn. 2007. "What's in the Box?" In *90 World-Class Activities by 90 World-Class Trainers*, edited by Elaine Biech, 94–96. San Francisco: Pfeiffer.

Rohnke, Karl. 2004. *Funn 'n Games.* Dubuque, IA: Kendall Hunt.

Sikes, Sam. 1998. *Executive Marbles and Other Team Building Activities.* Tulsa, OK: Learning Unlimited Corporation.

Sugar, Steve, and George Takacs. 2000. *Games That Teach Teams: 21 Activities to Super-Charge Your Group!* San Francisco: Pfeiffer.

Tuckman, Bruce W., and Mary Ann C. Jensen. 1977. "Stages of Small-Group Development Revisited."

Wujec, Tom. 2010. www.Marshmallowchallenge.com

Recommended Reading

Chrissley, Darlene. 2012. *Conversations for Power and Possibility: Four Simple Conversations to Transform Your Life and Change the World*. Toronto: BPS Books.

Mitsch, D. J., and Barry Mitsch. 2010. *Team Advantage: The Complete Coaching Guide for Team Transformation*. San Francisco: Pfeiffer.

Scannell, Mary. 2010. *Big Book of Conflict Resolution Games*. New York: McGraw-Hill.
Learn to turn conflicts into opportunities for collaboration, all while building trust and respect.

Scannell, Mary, and Ed Scannell. 2009. *Big Book of Team-Motivating Games*. New York: McGraw-Hill.
Games to increase engagement, improve communication, and get your team fired up.

Scannell, Mary, and Jim Cain, 2012. *Big Book of Low-Cost Training Games*. New York: McGraw-Hill.
Cost-effective activities and exercises that deliver outstanding results.

Scannell, Mary, Michael Abrams, and Mike Mulvihill. 2012. *Big Book of Virtual Team-Building Games*. New York: McGraw-Hill.
Activities to connect your team members, even when they are separated by space and time.

Scannell, Mary, and Mike Mulvihill. 2012. *Big Book of Brainstorming Games*. New York: McGraw-Hill.
Unleash your team's creative power with games that engage all personality types.

About the Authors

 **Mary Scannell** is an experiential team coach and elite trainer known for her engaging, high-energy style. She has worked with all levels of staff, and her programs range from facilitating retreats for senior executives to providing virtual and on-site sessions for newly formed teams. Her expertise spans a wide variety of areas, including communication, change management, conflict-to-collaboration, customer service, and team building.

Mary loves using games to infuse training with energy and purpose and is the author or co-author of several books in the Big Book Series, including *The Book of Team-Motivating Games*, *The Big Book of Conflict Resolution Games*, and *The Big Book of Low-Cost Training Games*. She is a member of the American Society for Training and Development and the Association for Experiential Education.

Mary lives in Colorado, where she is surrounded by brilliant coaches and beautiful mountains. You can connect with Mary by email at Mary@MaryScannell.com.

 **Mike Mulvihill** is the founder of PossibiliTEAMS, a team-building and training company offering fun and innovative team events to traditional corporate groups as well as virtual work teams around the globe. PossibiliTEAMS is the first company to offer a full lineup of team-building activities using virtual world technology. Mike has worked with teams throughout the United States, Europe, and Latin America, creating and facilitating team-building sessions for hundreds of organizations, ranging from Fortune 500 companies to small businesses, nonprofit groups, and government agencies.

Mike has worked with clients that include Liberty Mutual Insurance, Pearson Digital Learning, Bank of America, McKinsey & Company, Charles Schwab, American Express, UPS, Motorola, Discover Financial Services, the Federal Highway Administration, and many more.

He is co-author of *The Big Book of Virtual Teambuilding Games* and *The Big Book of Brainstorming Games* and is a member of the Society for Human Resource Management as well as the American Society for Training and Development. He received his bachelor's degree in organizational communication from Arizona State University.

Connect with Mike at PossibiliTEAMS at (888) 225–3610, or by email at Mike@PossibiliTEAMS.com.

Joanne Schlosser, MBA, ACC, SPHR, is a consultant and certified coach with extensive business experience. Her passion is coaching leaders and their teams to achieve extraordinary results. Joanne served as director of Talent and Organizational Effectiveness for Banner Health, where she was instrumental in the creation and execution of the coaching program, which won the 2012 International Prism Award for coaching excellence from the International Coach Federation. She wrote "Coaching: An Innovative Approach to Developing Leaders at Banner Health," published in August 2011 by the *International Journal of Coaching in Organizations*.

In addition to providing leadership coaching for high-potential managers, mid-level leaders, senior executives, and physicians, she has delivered thousands of dynamic, engaging presentations, workshops, and retreats. Joanne is an accomplished speaker, trainer, and former chapter president of the National Speakers Association, Arizona Chapter.

As a coach, consultant and speaker, Joanne has delighted over 100 entities from Fortune 500 to small businesses, government agencies, and associations. Clients include: Walt Disney World, Vanguard Health Systems, Hyatt, Berlex Laboratories, and University of Phoenix.

For more information or to schedule Joanne to work with your team, please contact Rising Stars Leadership Coaching at 480-840-6024, email Joanne@RisingStarsCoach.com, or visit www.RisingStarsCoach.com.